PONDMASTER

A practical guide to building and maintaining a

KOI POND

KEITH HOLMES AND TONY PITHAM

INTERPET PUBLISHING

Authors

Keith Holmes and Tony Pitham are Manager and MD of Koi Water Barn, the largest Koi Company in the UK. They have a wealth of experience in all aspects of the hobby, from koi pond construction to koi health and appreciation. Tony is a frequent visitor to Japan to purchase high-grade koi and is a regular judge at the Shinkokai All Japan Show. Both write regularly for koi magazines worldwide.

© 2002 Interpet Publishing,
Vincent Lane, Dorking, Surrey, RH4 3YX, England.

ISBN: 978-1-84286-063-2
This reprint 2008

Credits

Created and designed: Ideas into Print,
New Ash Green, Kent DA3 8JD, England.
Production management: Consortium, Poslingford,
Suffolk CO10 8RA, England.
Print production: Sino Publishing House Ltd., Hong Kong.
Printed and bound in China. Reprinted 2007

Below: Even as you approach the side of the pond, koi will swim to the surface in the expectation of being fed, one of the most satisfying experiences for both you and your handsome 'pets'.

Contents

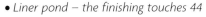

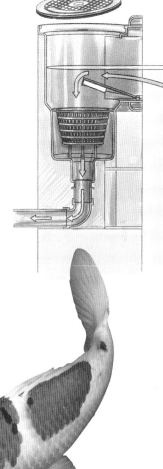

A formal koi pond softened with planting creates a practical and attractive garden feature.

Part One

Accepting the challenge

If you are reading this book, you probably already have some form of pond, but you have been bitten by the 'koi bug' and are ready to accept the challenge of becoming a koi-keeper. Uppermost in your mind will be a burning desire to build a stunning pond in which to house your future collection of these magnificent ornamental fish. But do not rush! Building a koi pond raises a vast array of questions that you need to answer long before you start digging a hole in your garden. The opening section of this book provides the initial advice and practical guidance you need to get you started. Here you will find help on choosing the right location, deciding on the type of pond you want and an insight into the bewildering variety of equipment associated with the hobby, from filter systems and media to pumps, valves, pipes and heating equipment.

If you are serious about your new koi pond, it must be gravity-fed, and the full implications of this will be highlighted later. However, before you make that decision you must consider the extent to which you wish to pursue your new hobby. Remember that even though you may have the space to accommodate a 12x6m (40x20ft) pond, you will also need to house the large filter system required to run it, buy all the necessary equipment, afford the running and maintenance costs associated with a pond of this size, and even catch the fish once they are in the pond! It is easy to dream beyond your means.

You must look seriously at your garden and your budget and install a pond that not only fits in the space, but is affordable in the long term. You will derive far more enjoyment from a manageable 9,000-litre (2,000-gallon) pond than from a badly designed 180,000-litre (40,000-gallon) one.

Once you have made these vital decisions, you are ready to begin reading and gaining an insight into the methods and products needed to build and maintain a koi pond. One final point to make is that by deciding to build a koi pond you are entering a whole new world of technical terms and products. If you are unsure, do seek advice from friendly hobbyists or speak to your local koi dealer, who will be more than willing to offer guidance.

A garden pond or a koi pond?

There are some vital differences between a 'garden pond' and a 'koi pond'. It is important to understand these distinctions before we look more closely at how to build a koi pond.

What is a garden pond?

A garden pond is literally a water feature that enhances the appearance of a garden and supports a wide range of plants and wildlife that share the watery environment. When you create a garden pond you can choose from a host of aquatic plants to soften the edges of the construction and provide colour and interest the whole year through. Around the perimeter of the pond you can feature moisture-loving plants, such as hostas and primulas, that will thrive in constantly damp soil. In the shallow water over a planting shelf or lapping onto a 'beach', you can grow a huge selection of marginal plants, from the bright yellow blooms of spring-flowering *Caltha* to the elegant spikes of irises and tall stems of reeds and rushes that continue their display into the autumn months. And in the deepest parts of the pond, you can enjoy the elegance of water lilies, surely the most magnificent of aquatic plants.

Into this 'jungle' of plants and water, you can introduce goldfish and other hardy pond fish. These will thrive and survive throughout the year and be joined by native creatures, such as frogs, toads, newts, water beetles and dragonflies, that will make themselves at home in your pond environment. And the added bonus is that you can create this diverse and successful habitat without worrying too much about a minimum overall size or water depth, and

without too much in the way of complicated life-support systems. Yes, you will need a filter and a water pump if you want to sustain quite a few fish or build a waterfall and fountain, but to a large extent a well set up garden pond is a self-sustaining system.

What is a koi pond?

Like a garden pond, a koi pond is also a hole in the ground filled with water, but there the resemblance ends. A koi pond has a single purpose: to provide a suitable environment for keeping koi. And because

Above: A well-planted garden pond in midsummer, with the water lilies in flower and the goldfish active and hungry. A garden pond can support a wide range of plants that would not survive the attentions of koi.

koi are fast-growing fish that produce a great deal of waste, the main aim is to create and maintain a large volume of clean, well-oxygenated water in which they can flourish and show off their colours. A koi pond should be at least 1.5m (4ft) deep and to keep the water clean it must have a filter system that can cope with the heavy demands the koi will put upon it. Unfortunately, since koi will disrupt any plants in the pond, the 'clean functionality' of a koi pond cannot be softened by the addition of aquatic plants, unless they are grown in protected zones.

Of course, this does not mean that a koi pond should not please the eye and become an attractive garden feature, but it will generally take up more space than a garden pond and require more services and equipment, such as the filter system, water supply, drainage pipework, electricity supply for pumps, heaters and water treatment devices, and generally be more 'complicated' and functional.

A successful koi pond is basically a water treatment plant with fish swimming in it. If you can make it look good at the same time, then you have succeeded on all fronts.

Right: Although surrounded by planting, the water of this koi pond is typically clear of aquatic plants. The water is filtered to a higher standard than in a garden pond in order to cope with the large amounts of waste produced by the fish.

Below: An echo of Japan – the home of koi – is commonly seen in Western koi ponds. This wooden bridge and pagoda add an oriental flavour to an informal koi pond photographed in spring.

Once you have decided to build a koi pond, the next most important decision is where to put it. Besides purely aesthetic considerations, there are a number of other factors that will influence your choice of location. Here we consider them in turn.

What lies beneath?

Building a koi pond involves a major excavation of the soil in your garden. Clearly you need to check what lies beneath the surface before you start digging. The main 'obstacles' will be water supply and gas pipework, electricity cables, rainwater soakaways,

Below: Before you start excavating, find out as much as you can about what might already be in the ground. Here, a drainpipe from a previous pond has been uncovered.

manholes and tree roots. You may need to look at your original building plans or consult local utility companies for advice on the location of services to your property.

Connections to utilities

Having discovered where the water, gas and electricity supplies run in your garden so that you can avoid disrupting them when you excavate the pond, you also need to make sure the pond is conveniently located for connection to them. A koi pond will need a water supply for filling and topping up, a drainage system for carrying away waste water, an electricity supply to power pumps and other essential equipment, and possibly a gas supply if you plan to include a gas-fired water heating system. If your first choice of location makes it difficult to install these essential services, then think again. It may be better to choose a compromise location to avoid having to dig up that newly laid patio simply to provide power. And always think ahead; you may wish to upgrade your system in the future and you should establish that electricity cables, for example, will be able to carry a higher load if you install more pumps or additional water treatment devices.

Gaining access to the site

Even a relatively small koi pond entails the shifting of a great deal of soil. Unless you enjoy the back-breaking process of digging the cavity out by hand, you will want to use a mechanical excavator. You can hire small diggers that will fit through boundary openings as narrow as 1m (39in). Check that your site

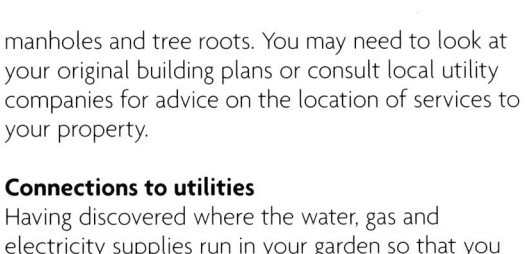

Above: Narrow access points to your garden can cause serious problems during the pond building process. Small excavators such as this are the ideal solution for restricted sites.

allows access for such a machine and that you have space to remove any excavated soil that you are not keeping to make a rockery or waterfall feature in the garden. You may need to remove some fence panels during the building process to improve access. If you are not confident about using a mechanical digger, you can hire one complete with an operator to carry out the main excavation work. Although relatively expensive, this will be money well spent to get the project underway.

Position in the garden

Of course, the main point in building a koi pond is so that you can enjoy it. Therefore, choose a location that allows you to view the fish easily on a day-to-day basis. And you will need to provide easy access

Below: This koi pond at the bottom of the garden is easily viewed through patio windows from the house, which is set at a higher level.

for routine maintenance, even during the cold, wet days of winter. So avoid building the pond in that remote corner of the garden that you rarely use; otherwise you will remember why you never use it! Also consider the position of established trees in the garden. These and other plants may shed leaves into the water that will block up surface skimmers during the autumn and winter. Left in the water, they will rot down and cause pollution problems for the fish. Where suitable, place the pond reasonably close to the house so that you can watch the fish from your window on colder days. But if you do this, take care not to undermine the foundations of the house or any nearby buildings during the building process.

Below: An indoor pond offers many benefits, including easy access and total environmental control. This stylish 36,000-litre (8,000-gallon) pond is heated by a gas boiler.

Above: A corner can be an ideal location for a koi pond. The boundaries can be disguised with a bamboo fence or the essence of a Japanese teahouse, as here.

What type of pond construction?

Depending on your preference and your budget, you can build a koi pond in two main ways: lining the cavity with a flexible sheet of specially formulated plastic or rubber material or building up the walls of the pond from concrete blocks on a concrete foundation slab and then lining this with a flexible liner, painting it with a pond sealant or bonding sheets of fibreglass matting onto the walls with an adhesive resin. Here we consider these options in more detail.

A simple liner pond
Lining the excavation with pond liner is the simplest approach. The advantages of this method are that it is quick, easy, relatively cheap and suitable for informal shapes (although you may need to sort out the overlaps and creases carefully to avoid creating pockets where debris could be trapped). The main disadvantage is that you must take extra care when cutting and sealing holes in the liner for exit and entry points of pipework associated with drains and pumped water returns. Before installing a liner, be sure to cover the surface of the excavation with underlay to cushion and protect the liner from any stones or sharp fragments in the soil. It is best to use a polyester underlay rather than an old carpet, which may rot away and stop protecting the liner after a few years. You can buy liners in various formulations and thicknesses. The most suitable ones are 0.5-1.0mm thick and made from plasticised PVC, bonded composite materials, EPDM, and butyl rubber. Buy one with a lifetime guarantee and source it from a reputable dealer who will honour the warranty.

If you are planning to build a simple liner pond, consider constructing a concrete collar in the shape of the pond before you start digging. This should be at least 23cm(9in) wide and deep and will stabilise the edge of the cavity as you dig down. It will also form a firm foundation for the edging stones or slabs around the finished pond. (See pages 36-45 for a step-by-step guide to building a liner pond.)

A concrete block-built pond
The first step in this construction method involves laying down a slab of concrete as a base, usually with reinforcing steel mesh embedded within it. The walls of the pond are then built up using standard 45x23cm (18x9in) pierced concrete blocks, also with steel reinforcement in the form of steel rods passing vertically through the cavities of the blocks. The inside surface of the block wall is then coated with a cement render. To increase the overall strength of the construction, it is best to add strands of fibreglass to the render before applying it to the

Left: This impressive liner pond of 34,000 litres (7,500 gallons) has one bottom drain linked to a gravity-fed filter system consisting of a vortex and a three-chambered filter.

Above: This deep pond under construction has been rendered and will be fibreglassed. There are four bottom drains (two in view) in dished zones that aid drainage. The pumped returns are angled for good water circulation.

walls. This so-called fibremix can increase the strength of the render by ten times. Ideally, burn off any protruding strands of fibreglass as the render dries to create a smooth finish.

Lining or sealing a block-built pond

Once the block shell is complete – and even without rendering the surface – you can line the cavity with a pond liner. Not only does the rigid shell make it easier to fit pipework to the flexible lining material but it also allows the use of box-welded liners that exactly fit the construction without unsightly creases.

An alternative and simple way of finishing the surface of a rendered block-built pond is to paint it with a sealant. Various products are available, usually

in various colours. It is vital to ensure that the render is completely dry before you apply the sealant and to pick a day with good weather so that you can rely on dry conditions as you apply the three or four coats that some types of sealant need. Allow plenty of time for the task, because you need to apply each new coat before the previous one has dried.

If you want to achieve the best possible result, seal the surface with sheets of fibreglass matting. This method is relatively expensive – although becoming cheaper – but it does create a tough pond lining that will last for many years. It is not a technique suitable for beginners, or indeed for most koi hobbyists, and so it is best to engage a reputable professional company to carry out the work. Most koi dealers will have a fibreglasser inhouse or be able

to engage the services of a specialist team. If you opt for this method, remember to establish exactly what you will get for your money, as the quality of the materials used is usually reflected in the price.

Whichever method you choose to line or seal a block-built pond, the quality of the finished result will always rely on the sturdiness of the basic construction. Get this right, and you have the makings of a strong and durable koi pond.

Below: This koi pond is constructed of pierced concrete blocks, which have been rendered and then fibreglassed to create a smooth and durable surface. The pond has a capacity of 25,000 litres (5,600 gallons) and is home to a superb selection of koi.

Pump-fed or gravity-fed pond?

Having decided on the construction method and location of your new pond, it is now time to start thinking about filtration. But before you even decide on the most suitable type of filter system, you must decide how you plan to get the water from the pond to the filter and back again. Basically, you have two choices: a pump-fed system or a gravity-fed system. Here we look at these strategies in more detail so that you can decide which one to use. Both systems have their advantages and disadvantages, but for a koi pond a gravity-fed setup is the one to choose.

Pump-fed filter systems

In this system, dirty water is pumped from the pond to an external filter and 'clean' water returns to the pond by gravity. The first critical disadvantage of this arrangement is that because the pump is in the pond, it is liable to become blocked and needs frequent cleaning. New pumps are continually being produced that will handle larger and larger solids, but inevitably they too will become blocked, perhaps with blanketweed or larger debris. The second main problem with a pump-fed system is that the external filter must be higher than the water level in the pond so that clean water can flow back under gravity. This not only means that the returning water has little or no pressure (to power venturis, for example) but also the pump needs to be powerful enough to lift the water up into the filter system.

From the cosmetic angle, an external filter sitting next to your newly landscaped pond and garden can be extremely unsightly and difficult to disguise. The

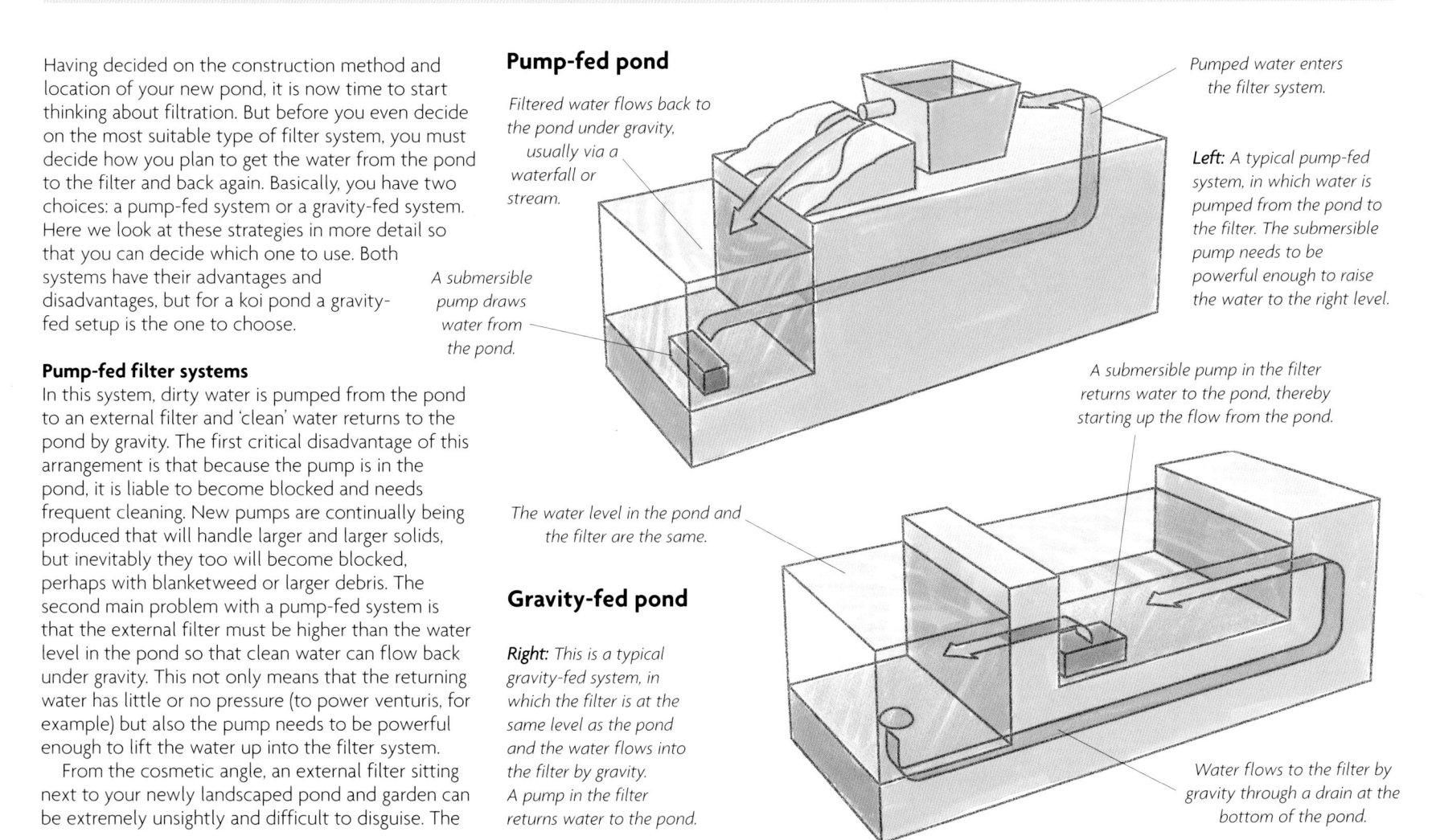

Pump-fed pond

Filtered water flows back to the pond under gravity, usually via a waterfall or stream.

Pumped water enters the filter system.

Left: A typical pump-fed system, in which water is pumped from the pond to the filter. The submersible pump needs to be powerful enough to raise the water to the right level.

A submersible pump draws water from the pond.

A submersible pump in the filter returns water to the pond, thereby starting up the flow from the pond.

The water level in the pond and the filter are the same.

Gravity-fed pond

Right: This is a typical gravity-fed system, in which the filter is at the same level as the pond and the water flows into the filter by gravity. A pump in the filter returns water to the pond.

Water flows to the filter by gravity through a drain at the bottom of the pond.

Above: This large, gravity-fed pond supports a good collection of koi that are completely at home in their mature garden setting. The filter runs alongside the pond under decking.

Above: A pump-fed system can incorporate a waterfall to hide the external filter raised above the pond water level and to provide an attractive feature for the water returning to the pond by gravity.

pipework carrying water from the filter back to the pond must be level or sloping towards the pond. As this water is at a very low pressure, you will need to use a large-bore pipe to prevent the filter filling up quicker than it can empty. This return pipe may need to be 110mm (4in) in diameter and if it connects to a filter some distance from the pond this, too, can be a difficult feature to hide.

Despite these disadvantages, a pump-fed filter does have the merits of being easy to install and relatively cheap. Remember, however, that you will never be able to pump all the waste from the bottom of the pond and that you will need a vacuum cleaning device to do this effectively. Ease of construction and installation is a trade-off against the increased amount and expense of maintenance once the system is up and running.

Gravity-fed filter systems

In a gravity-fed filter system the water in the filter is at the same level as that in the pond. A wide-bore pipe drains water from the bottom of the pond into the filter. This means that the filter can be buried next to the pond, or if the pond is raised, the filter is also raised by the same amount. In ponds up to 18,000 litres (4,000 gallons) capacity, a single drain in the centre of the pond base will be sufficient. It is best to slope the base towards the drain to help water flow. In larger ponds, two or more drains will be needed and here it is advisable to divide the base into separate zones, each sloped towards their respective drains. The pipe connecting the pond base to the filter is usually 110mm (4in) in diameter.

Once the pond is filled with water it will flow into and also fill the filter system. To set up a circulation, a submersible pump is placed in the final filter chamber or an external pump is fitted in the pipework after the filter system. The pump propels cleaned water back into the pond and dirty water from the pond base flows into the filter by gravity to take its place. Because the pump handles filtered water, it is unlikely to clog and needs very little maintenance. Also, it is easy to reach the pump for maintenance, repair or replacement. Because the water is pumped back to the pond, the return pipes can be relatively small (42-50mm/1.5-2.0in diameter is normal) and these can be positioned below water level, resulting in no visible pipework.

A major advantage of a gravity-fed system is that the water flowing away from the pond through the bottom drain carries the waste through to the filter system. As a bonus, the pond contains no pumps or other devices that could disrupt good water flow or present obstructions that could damage the koi.

From the appearance point of view, a gravity-fed system enables you to bury the pond filtration equipment – perhaps concealed beneath removable wooden decking panels – and to locate it for easy access. Although such a filter system entails extra work and expense at the installation stage, these are more than outweighed by the benefit the system provides you and your koi.

You may be confused by the wide range of filter systems available at your local dealer and advertised in the pages of the koi hobby and water gardening magazines. Which one you choose depends on whether you favour a pump-fed or gravity-fed system, how much space you have available, how much you want to spend and your personal preference about the design and specification of the system. Here, we try to make sense of all those bewildering options by dividing filters into categories based on their size and form.

Single chamber filters

As the name suggests, this type of filter consists of one chamber, normally made from a plastic tank and supplied with a combination of media, such as aquarock and foam. It usually has a spray bar through which the incoming water is pumped at the top of the unit. The water then flows down through the media and returns to the pond through an outlet pipe near the base. These filters offer more of a 'quick fix' rather than a long-term solution, and are not suited to the demands of a koi pond. This is principally due to the fact that they are pump fed (i.e. supplied with water from a submersible pump in the pond) and the media inside the filter body cannot handle the waste loads put on them by koi.

Multichamber filters

These consist of between three and eight chambers, depending on the pond volume they are intended to filter. Their main advantage is that you can place different filter media in each chamber. Thus, in the

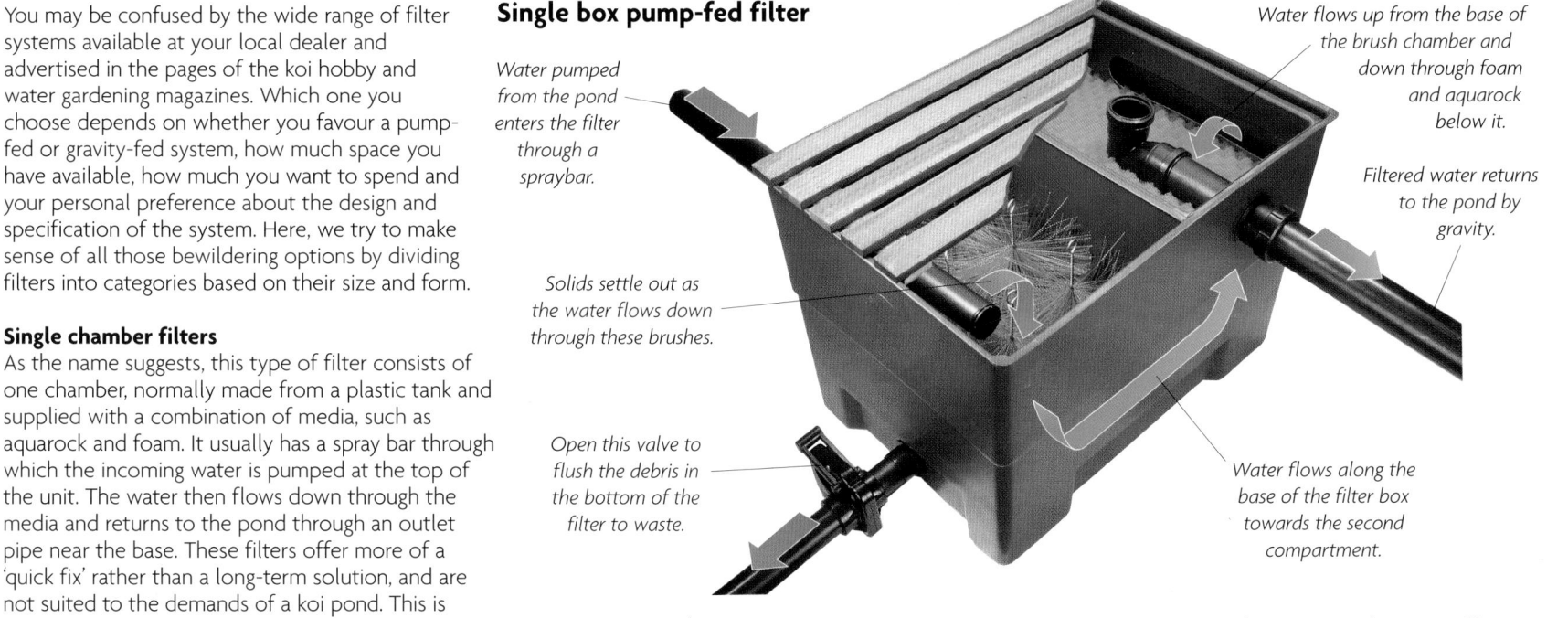

Single box pump-fed filter

Water pumped from the pond enters the filter through a spraybar.

Solids settle out as the water flows down through these brushes.

Open this valve to flush the debris in the bottom of the filter to waste.

Water flows up from the base of the brush chamber and down through foam and aquarock below it.

Filtered water returns to the pond by gravity.

Water flows along the base of the filter box towards the second compartment.

first chamber it is normal to have a medium, such as brushes, that is good at straining out heavy waste, and in the last chamber a medium designed to trap very fine particles in a 'water polishing' final stage. The chambers in between can contain various types of media, mainly to carry out biological filtration.

Multichamber filters are normally made from heavy duty plastic or fibreglass and in most cases incorporate drainage points on each chamber for the easy removal of waste. Multichamber units offer an

ideal starting point when you are choosing a filter system for your new koi pond. The only drawback with these filters is that they are moulded as one unit and those with several chambers need a large and especially long space to accommodate them.

Vortex chambers

These are not complete filter systems on their own, but they do offer an efficient way of dealing with heavy waste in the initial stages of filtration. Before

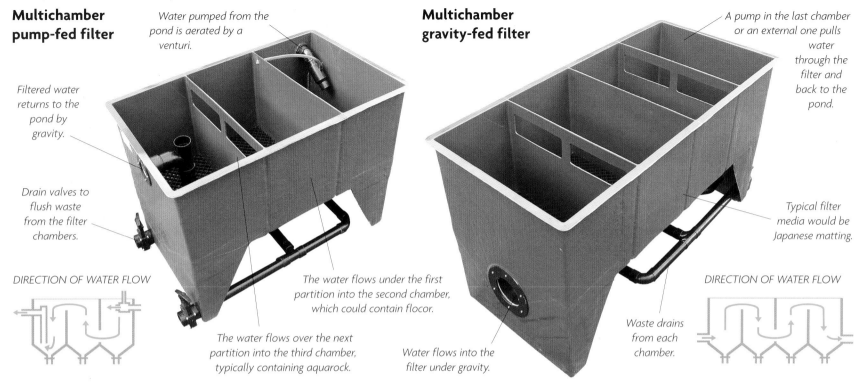

Multichamber pump-fed filter

Water pumped from the pond is aerated by a venturi.

Filtered water returns to the pond by gravity.

Drain valves to flush waste from the filter chambers.

DIRECTION OF WATER FLOW

The water flows over the next partition into the third chamber, typically containing aquarock.

The water flows under the first partition into the second chamber, which could contain flocor.

Multichamber gravity-fed filter

A pump in the last chamber or an external one pulls water through the filter and back to the pond.

Typical filter media would be Japanese matting.

Waste drains from each chamber.

DIRECTION OF WATER FLOW

Water flows into the filter under gravity.

we consider how a vortex chamber can be combined with other filter systems, let us see how they work and why they represent one of the most revolutionary devices currently available for koi pond filtration. If you are serious about keeping koi, you should definitely include a vortex chamber in your filter setup.

A vortex chamber is a very simple filter unit that makes use of a natural physical force. A vortex is a whirling mass of water – a whirlpool is a fast-moving example. The easiest way of creating a vortex is to spin water in a circular container. Stirring a liquid in a cup creates a miniature vortex. In the koi world, a vortex chamber consists of a cylinder – the bigger the better – in which a circulating flow of water is created by introducing the water at an angle so that it strikes the inner curved surface of the cylinder. The aim in a vortex chamber is to create a very slow-moving circulation so that any solid particles held in suspension settle out by gravity and collect in the base of the chamber. To facilitate the settlement process, the bottom section of the chamber is

shaped into a funnel that leads down to a central drain. Opening a valve connected to this allows the accumulated waste to be flushed away. The larger the vessel, the further the water has to travel before it moves into the next filtration chamber. It is important to control the flow rate from your pump to achieve the most efficient settlement of waste in a vortex chamber; the higher the flow rate, the less efficient the unit becomes.

Because of how it works, it is clear that a vortex chamber operates best as the first part of a gravity-fed filter system, in which the water flows slowly from the pond into the filter through a large-bore pipe. If it was part of a pump-fed filter system, the higher pressure of the incoming water would set up too fast a spin in the vortex chamber for there to be any useful settlement effect. Also, the swirling current could disturb any solid waste that did collect in the base.

Multichamber filters with a vortex

A vortex chamber can be used with a multichamber filter system in two ways. It can be an integral part of a moulded unit or simply added as a separate 'front end' to a multichamber system. The advantages of using a built-in vortex are that no additional pipework is needed and installation is straightforward. However, do bear in mind that such a system may be awkwardly long. Adding a separate vortex does at least allow for a degree of flexibility in positioning it in relation to the main filter unit.

However it is incorporated, a vortex brings the same benefits in removing a large amount of solid waste and thus freeing up one of the subsequent chambers and its media to do another job. The efficient removal of solid waste not only reduces maintenance on the other filter chambers – only the vortex will need regular draining – but it also allows one more chamber to contain a much-needed biological filter medium (see page 20).

Vortex chamber

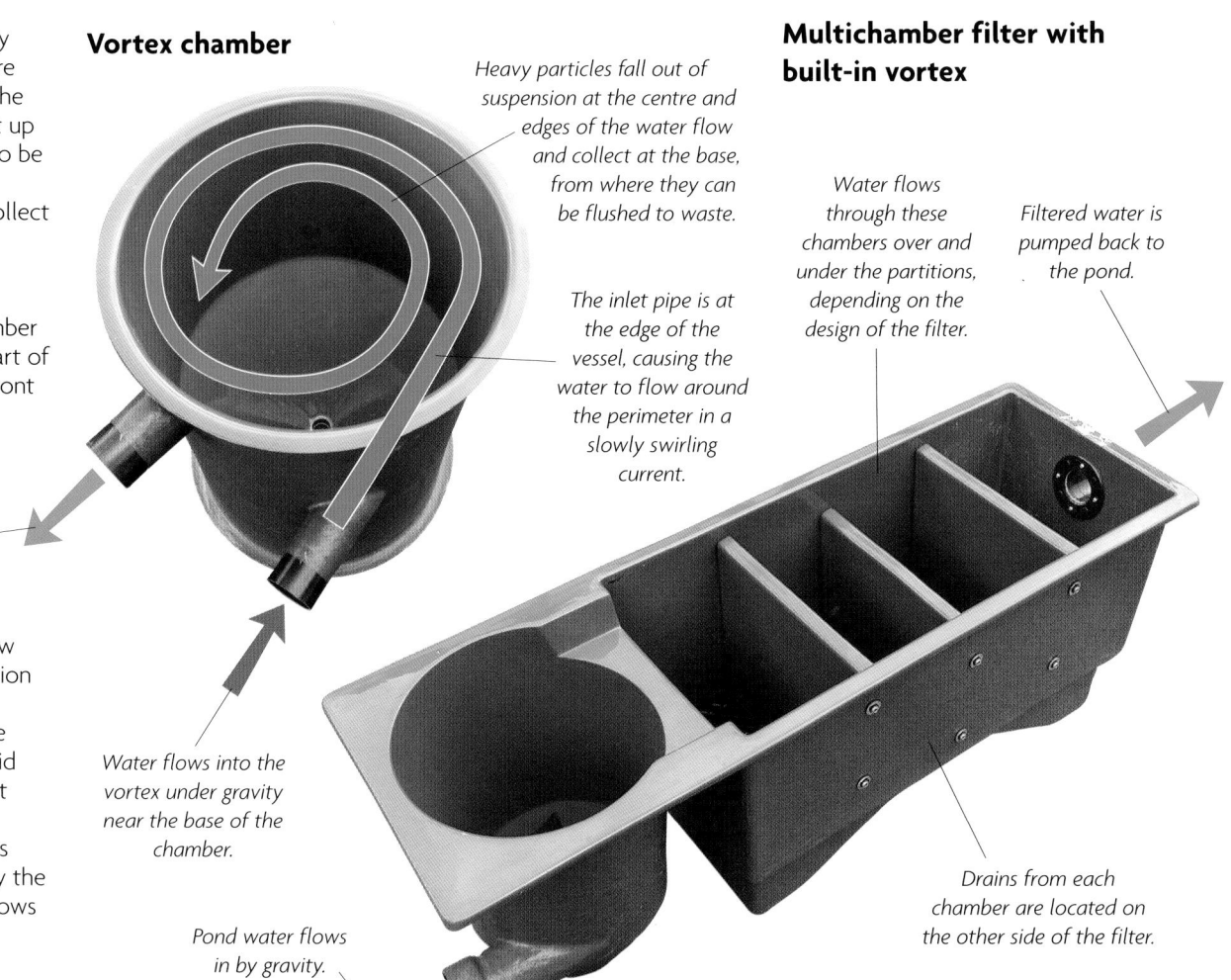

Heavy particles fall out of suspension at the centre and edges of the water flow and collect at the base, from where they can be flushed to waste.

The inlet pipe is at the edge of the vessel, causing the water to flow around the perimeter in a slowly swirling current.

Water free of heavy solids flows out at a higher level and into the first media chamber.

Water flows into the vortex under gravity near the base of the chamber.

Pond water flows in by gravity.

Multichamber filter with built-in vortex

Water flows through these chambers over and under the partitions, depending on the design of the filter.

Filtered water is pumped back to the pond.

Drains from each chamber are located on the other side of the filter.

Multichamber vortex filters

These are moulded units with cylindrical vortex-like chambers rather than the more usual square or rectangular ones. Although the media contained in the chambers will prevent a vortex water flow, many people consider that using cylindrical chambers prevents dead spots that can impede good flow in more conventional designs.

Multiple single chambers

This is the most flexible option, enabling you to configure your own filter system from individual chambers linked together. It is best to choose vortex chambers, even though only one will be used as such. The main disadvantage of this approach is that you will need to connect the chambers with the necessary pipework and valves. However, the overwhelming bonus is that you can position the chambers to suit your space. If you have an L-shaped area, you can arrange the units in the same way. And, of course, you can add units to increase the filter capacity as you increase the size or stocking level of your pond. (The block-built pond featured on pages 46-59 incorporates this type of filter system.)

An added benefit is that you can control the flow of water through the system. Ideally, it is best to have the water flowing up through the medium in each chamber, whereas in premoulded multichamber systems you are restricted to the flow pattern provided by the manufacturer.

Final thoughts on filters

Here we have considered the main types of filters available although, of course, there are many variations. At this point, it is probably clear to you that the best option is to choose a gravity-fed filter system incorporating a vortex chamber. If your pond

Multiple single chambers

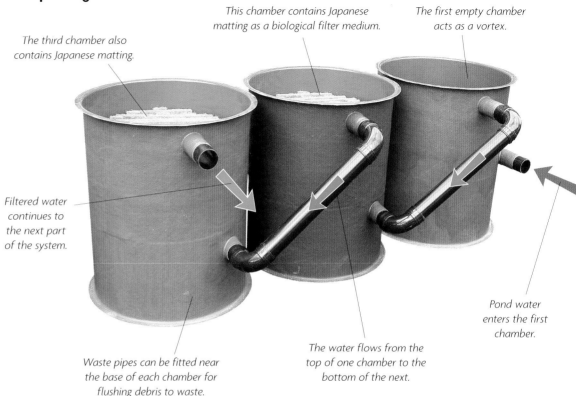

The third chamber also contains Japanese matting.

This chamber contains Japanese matting as a biological filter medium.

The first empty chamber acts as a vortex.

Filtered water continues to the next part of the system.

Waste pipes can be fitted near the base of each chamber for flushing debris to waste.

The water flows from the top of one chamber to the bottom of the next.

Pond water enters the first chamber.

has two bottom drains, it is worth installing a separate filter system for each drain. This will enable you to carry out vital maintenance work on one system while keeping the other one running. It will also give you a backup should a pump fail in one of the systems. You may think that installing two filters seems extravagant, but at least each one can be smaller than a single one.

Whatever type of filter system you choose for your pond, be sure to allow enough room for it in your garden. The classic mistake is to build a pond with a capacity of 45,000 litres (10,000 gallons) and then realise that you will need a quarter of that area for a suitable filter. Do your homework first and you will have a filter system that is efficient, not too obtrusive and easy to maintain.

What type of media?

At the same time as deciding which type of filter system to install, you should also be thinking about the filter media to use. There are many types available but all perform one or both of the following functions:

Mechanical filtration – literally trapping solid wastes and removing them from the water flow.

Biological filtration – providing a large surface area to support the growth of beneficial bacteria that break down pollutants in the water.

Before finally choosing the media, consider the following questions. What job does the medium do best? Will it trap solids or foster biological filtration by supporting millions of beneficial bacteria? The answer to this crucial question will guide you in placing each medium in the most appropriate stage of the filter system. Also consider how easy the medium is to work with. Is it heavy and will this put you off cleaning it? And remember to think about the amount of media you will need; a large pond may require a substantial amount of filter media to keep it clean. Also make sure that the direction of water flow through your system matches the way the particular medium works best. With these questions buzzing around in your mind, the photos and associated captions here provide a visual survey of the filter media you will find at your local koi centre. If you are still unsure, your dealer will advise you on the best media for your particular system.

Bacballs
These plastic balls provide a very large surface area for bacteria to colonise and so are ideal for biological filtration. They are easy to work with and clean, and allow a good flow of water through the filter. Avoid using them in the early stages of a filter system where they may become clogged with solid waste. They are relatively expensive and you may need to use quite a few to fill a large filter chamber.

Flocor and bioflow
Flocor consists of cut pieces of ribbed plastic pipe, while bioflow is made from specifically moulded plastic sections with a larger surface area. Both types are lightweight (flocor will float; bioflow will not), easy to clean and good for biological filtration. Because of the way the cut sections lock together in a filter chamber, they do collect a certain amount of solid material and so can be used in the early stages of a system as a mechanical medium. Large amounts need a strong supporting grid.

Aquarock
This cheap medium is made from pieces of clay fired at very high temperatures (sintered) so that the outer layer has a very pitted texture and thus provides a large surface area for bacteria to colonise. Not surprisingly, it forms an excellent biological filter medium. Unfortunately, it will clog easily in dirty water but is often used in the last chamber as a final 'polishing' medium before the water is pumped back to the pond. It is very heavy, which makes cleaning hard work and also means that strong supports are needed to hold its weight.

Cut pieces of plastic pipe provide a lightweight biological and mechanical filter medium.

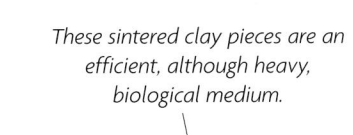

These ribbed plastic balls also provide a large surface area for beneficial bacteria.

These sintered clay pieces are an efficient, although heavy, biological medium.

Japanese matting

This has become the most widely used biological filter medium for koi ponds. It consists of hundreds of fibre strands formed into a sheet or 'mat', and is usually cut up and assembled as a cartridge as shown here. Used in this way, Japanese matting is self-supporting in a filter chamber and this reduces the need for filter grids. It is an excellent – if expensive – biological filter medium and in a system incorporating a vortex chamber may be the only media type needed. Avoid using it for mechanical filtration, as it clogs easily and repeated cleaning may weaken it to the point of disintegration.

Left: Japanese matting sheets cut and assembled into these 'cartridges' are one of the best types of biological filter medium available.

Right: Matala is a more rigid material than matting and is supplied in different grades. It can be used for mechanical as well as biological filtration.

Filter foam needs frequent cleaning but can help to improve water clarity.

Matala

Matala is a plastic matrix available as sheets of different thickness and density. It works as a biological filter like Japanese matting, but with appropriate use of the different grades can also provide effective mechanical filtration.

Foam sheets

Open-cell foam sheets of various grades can perform a useful role in filtering out small particles and thus improving water clarity before it returns to the pond. The foam sheets are simply laid over the top of other filter media in the system. It is not widely used for koi ponds and is best suited to small, single-chamber filters. Because it strains out the smallest debris, it has a high maintenance requirement and often needs replacing.

Brushes

The interlocking bristles of these brushes provide a simple way of trapping solids in the first stage of a filter system, preventing later biological stages from becoming clogged. Brushes are easy to clean and work with, which is just as well because they need frequent cleaning depending on the waste loads put upon them.

Brushes are an inexpensive, easy-to-clean mechanical filter medium. Available in a range of sizes.

Filter media combinations

A typical pump-fed multichamber system without a vortex could have the following sequence of media.

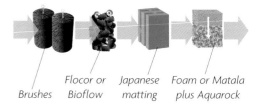

Brushes | Flocor or Bioflow | Japanese matting | Foam or Matala plus Aquarock

A gravity-fed system with a vortex could follow the same sequence, but the vortex normally makes the brushes unnecessary. The following media setup is considered by many koi-keepers to be the best.

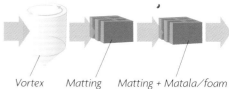

Vortex | Matting | Matting + Matala/foam

Pipes and valves

The pond and filter system are connected by pipework and it is vital to choose the correct types and sizes of pipes and valves to get your system running in the most efficient and reliable way. You will also need to consider where the pipework will run, whether it will be above or below the ground, have a long distance to run and be under pressure. Here we look at the options available and how to make the right choices from the outset.

Flexible hose

Flexible hose is the cheapest and most versatile type of pipework and is available in a range of bore sizes from 3 to 50mm(0.125-2in), although 38mm (1.5in) is normally the largest size used for koi ponds. The main advantages of flexible hose are that it is supplied in long lengths (normally up to 30m/100ft) and can easily cope with corners and irregular shapes. On the downside, it cannot be fitted with the valves and accessories widely used in the koi hobby and is normally used only where rigid pipework is unsuitable. A less serious problem is that flexible hoses can look very unsightly when installed.

Rigid pipework

Rigid plastic pipework is the best type to use for koi pond installations, especially gravity-fed systems. Using the right type and size of rigid pipework – normally the solvent-weld waste pipe – you can create a durable, efficient and 'professional-looking' system.

Below: Double union ball valves are used before and after this external pump. They will allow the pump to be replaced without cutting into the solvent-welded pipework around it.

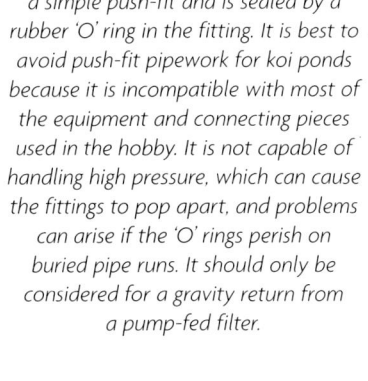

Push-fit pipe
This pipework connects by means of a simple push-fit and is sealed by a rubber 'O' ring in the fitting. It is best to avoid push-fit pipework for koi ponds because it is incompatible with most of the equipment and connecting pieces used in the hobby. It is not capable of handling high pressure, which can cause the fittings to pop apart, and problems can arise if the 'O' rings perish on buried pipe runs. It should only be considered for a gravity return from a pump-fed filter.

Solvent-weld pressure pipe
This pipe is designed for high-pressure applications and is not normally used on koi ponds, except in special situations. This would include connecting a pump to a sand filter, which operates under pressure. Pressure pipe has the same compatibility and ease-of-use advantages as waste pipe but is expensive and can be difficult to obtain – especially when you need it most!

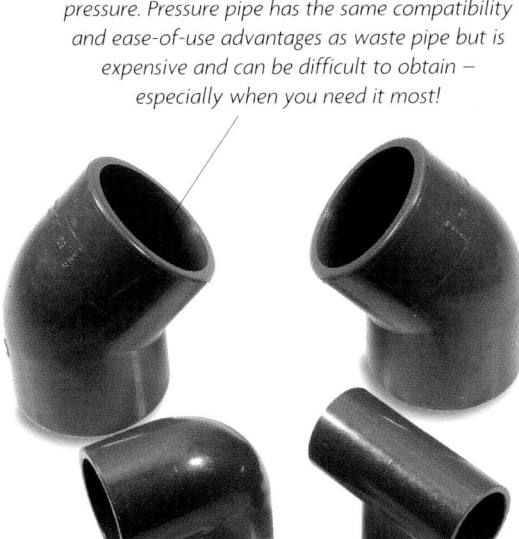

Using pipework

Whatever type of pipework you choose, always follow these simple rules:

Use the right pipe

Ensure that you use the correct type and size of pipe for each part of the system and that the pipes can handle the volume of water you want to put through them.

Do a dry run first

Before gluing solvent-weld connections, place the pipes and valves in position in a 'dry run' and mark all the pipework clearly. Once you have glued them together, you will never be able to separate the joints.

Match special components

If you are using any specialist equipment, such as sophisticated pumps and filtration devices, follow the manufacturer's recommendations for suitable pipework diameters. Generally speaking, the larger the pipe diameter, the lower the resistance and thus the lower the flow loss.

Use plenty of valves

Fit as many valves as possible so that you can isolate and replace faulty pumps and other devices without having to cut pipework. Fit a valve (normally a 110mm/4in slide or ball valve) before the filter so that you can isolate it from the pond for maintenance and purging pipes

Solvent-weld waste pipe

With this pipework, all connections are glued to give strong and clean joints. It is the most widely used type and common sizes in use include 110mm (4in) for the gravity feed from the bottom drain to the filter and 38mm (1.5in) for pumped returns. It is cheap, readily available and most of the valves, pumps and other pieces of pond equipment can be fitted with this type of pipework or easily adapted to fit. It is also compatible with a huge range of angle connectors and sockets commonly seen in plumbing shops and koi dealers.

110mm (4in)
Used for drains

82mm (3in)
Used for drains

50mm (2in)
Used for returns

38mm (1.5in)
Used for returns

Slide valve

This type of valve is inexpensive to install and ideal for off/on applications such as waste drainage. Once installed, it can be removed only by cutting the pipework or dismantling the valve.

Clear hose

Transparent plastic hose allows you to see water flowing through it but also allows sunlight to penetrate and cause algae to grow. After a time, algae will block the pipe and reduce flow rates. This hose is prone to kinking around tight bends.

Black-ribbed reinforced hose

This is just as flexible as clear plastic hose, but is much stronger and does not kink around bends. Being black, it does not allow algae growth to build up.

Double union ball valve

This relatively expensive type of valve can be used to regulate flow and has a threaded fitting (or union) on both sides so that it can be disconnected from the pipework. This enables the valve or the equipment connected to it to be easily replaced should problems arise.

Green clear reinforced /Heavy duty black hose

Stronger than normal reinforced hose and ideal for applications where it needs to be buried.

Choosing a pump

The water pump is the workhorse of every koi pond. There are two types: submersible and external. Which one you choose will depend largely on how your final system will run.

Submersible pumps

As the name suggests, submersible pumps are used underwater, either in the pond for a pump-fed system or in the last chamber of the filter system on a gravity-fed pond. Submersible pumps

Submersible pump

Water outlet

Pump motor

Plastic strainer housing contains a block of foam to prevent solids clogging the pump impeller.

With the foam removed, some pumps of this type can be used externally, providing the water is free from solids.

Water drawn into pump

Sump, or cellar, pump

Water outlet

Pump inlet grill limits size of solids entering.

Float switches off pump when it falls below the top of casing.

are widely available, relatively inexpensive, very easy to install and can have a warranty period of up to five years. However, they do have a number of disadvantages, the most serious being cleaning and maintenance. Since the pump is located in the pond or the last filter chamber, cleaning entails removing the unit. This can be time consuming, especially for pumps in the pond, where they are exposed to dirty water and prone to clogging. The frequency of cleaning depends on the style of pump you have; submersibles with a pre-filter foam block, for example, need regular maintenance to keep them running efficiently. New pumps are being developed that will handle solids up to 10mm across, but they will still need cleaning.

The positioning of submersible pumps can also cause problems. In the pond, they are an obstacle on which koi could damage themselves. In the last

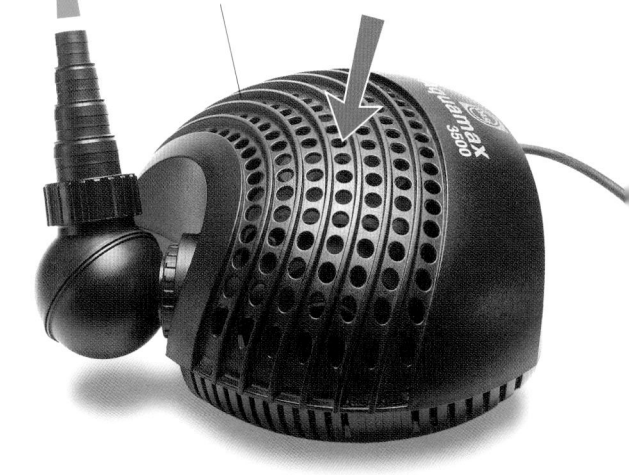

Submersible/external pump

This pump can handle 8mm (0.3in) solids and, with the casing removed, can be used externally.

Low-wattage external pump

These pumps are relatively cheap to run but do not deliver the same pressure as high-wattage models.

Water outflow

Water inlet. Normally a strainer basket is fitted here.

Pumped water outflow to pond or other treatment equipment.

Strainer basket prevents solids damaging pump impeller.

Pump motor

filter chamber, they take up valuable media space, which could mean having to increase the size of the filter to compensate.

External pumps

For a gravity-fed pond, an external pump is the best choice. The pump is placed after the filter system and so pumps clean filtered water back to the pond. This not only cuts down on maintenance but also makes access easy should any attention be necessary.

Single-purpose external pumps are normally large, robust units with the advantage of a straining basket to trap debris before it enters the pump impeller. They need to be sited under cover or in a weatherproof housing. Dual-purpose external pumps that can also be used in a submersible mode are

Water inlet from filter or surface skimmer.

High-wattage external pump

Mount external pumps in a dry, sheltered place.

usually smaller and when used out of the water are by design able to withstand wet weather conditions. Despite this welcome versatility, dual-purpose pumps may not be powerful enough to move the high volumes of water needed on large koi ponds or be able to maintain the water pressure to operate some specialist equipment.

These two factors of flow rate and water pressure capability are crucial considerations when choosing an external pump. Always choose a pump that will maintain a sufficient flow rate. Ideally, you will want to turn the whole pond volume over once every two hours. Check that the pump can cope with the flow loss caused by the height the water needs to reach and by restrictions caused by the pipework. Also check that the pump will be able to maintain the pressure necessary to operate all the 'extras' that you may wish to connect to your system. Finally, also think about the power consumption of your pump. Lower wattage pumps are becoming available that, although more expensive to buy, will repay their cost differential in lower running costs. Bear in mind, however, that lower wattage pumps may not generate the pressure you need and that you will need to buy a bigger model to achieve the optimum flow rate.

Heating a koi pond

Once restricted to 'top koi-keepers', pond heating has now become part of the wider hobby. One reason for this is that the necessary equipment is now more widely available and at a reasonable cost. The second reason is that most of the koi now being imported into cool temperate regions have not experienced the conditions of an unheated pond in the cold winter months. By 'pond heating' we mean not simply keeping the water ice free, but maintaining a minimum temperature of 12-14°C (54-57°F).

Heating reduces dangerous fluctuations in temperature and allows the koi to feed all year. If you are unsure about heating, it is worth considering that in the long term it could prevent many problems and safeguard the health of your potentially prize-winning collection. After all, the value of one good-quality koi could cover the cost of a simple heating system.

How to heat the water? There are two types of heating system widely used to heat a koi pond: direct electric heating and secondary systems using a heat exchanger connected to a gas or oil-fired boiler.

Direct electric heating

This is the easiest heating system to install and generally takes the form of an inline electric heater fitted in the pipe returning water to the pond in a gravity-fed system. Where an external pump is used the heater would normally be positioned after the

Control unit housing timer, thermostat and digital readout of water temperature.

Inline electric water heater

Efficient and simple to install, electric heaters are the easiest option for water heating.

The power lead connects to this unit, which in some models also houses the timer and thermostat.

Heated water out. The flow direction is normally controlled by a flow switch that turns the unit off if the water pump stops.

Cool water in

Probe in the pond monitors water temperature and relays this to the display and thermostat in the control unit.

pump. Depending on the ambient temperature of the water, allow one kilowatt of electrical power per 4,500 litres (1,000 gallons) of pond capacity. Ideally, choose the next most powerful heater so that it is not permanently on during severe periods of cold weather. Choose a model with a digital thermostat. These offer more precise control over the heating process and provide an accurate readout of the current water temperature. If you are not experienced, engage a qualified electrician to install any type of electric heating system.

Heat exchanger systems

Although more expensive to buy and install, systems that use a heat exchanger are more economical in terms of running costs, particularly on larger ponds. The heat exchanger – normally made of stainless steel – is literally a radiator that is fed with hot water heated in a boiler, which can be fuelled by gas, oil or bottled gas. Pond water is pumped through the exchanger and is heated by conduction as it passes over the hot water element inside. Water temperature is monitored by a probe in the pond connected to a digital thermostat that fires up the heating boiler when needed. If it is powerful enough, you can run the exchanger from your domestic heating system. Consult a qualified engineer to install such a system and take specialist advice if you plan to connect the pond heating setup to your home system.

Conserving heat

Whether you heat your pond or not, it is worth covering the pond, filter and pipework to reduce heat loss in cold conditions. This would keep the temperature up by as much as 2-3°C (3-5°F) and, if you are heating the water, help to keep the bills down. Do not make the covering airtight and be sure to uncover a small section at least once a day to allow any gases that have built up to escape.

Left: Covering the pond during the cold winter months is a good way of conserving heat. Zipped panels on this cover allow ventilation and access to the fish as needed.

Water inlet from filter system.

Heat exchanger for gas-fired boiler

A heat exchanger supplied with hot water from a boiler is a very cost-effective way of heating pond water. The exchanger is best mounted vertically.

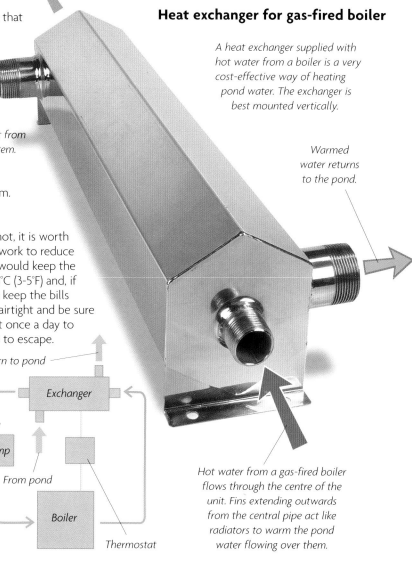

Warmed water returns to the pond.

Return to pond

Exchanger

Pump

From pond

Boiler

Thermostat

Hot water from a gas-fired boiler flows through the centre of the unit. Fins extending outwards from the central pipe act like radiators to warm the pond water flowing over them.

Other equipment

In addition to the main filtration system, there are many other items of equipment that you can add to your koi pond to improve water quality and facilitate maintenance. Here we look at the range of options available and explain briefly how they work.

Surface skimmers

A surface skimmer is an absolute must, rather than an optional extra. As the name suggests, this unit literally skims the top layer of water and removes leaves, dust and other debris floating on the surface. The most effective type of skimmer is built into the pond wall and so must be installed early in the construction phase. An external pump – either the main one or a dedicated one – pulls water through a strainer basket in the unit by drawing water into the mouth of the skimmer over a flap-type weir. It is a simple matter to remove and empty the strainer basket when necessary. It is important to position the skimmer in the pond where the water is flowing towards it so that the surface debris is carried into the mouth. For example, if you have a waterfall at one end, install the skimmer at the opposite end.

Aeration systems

Some way of introducing air into a koi pond is essential, principally to maintain dissolved oxygen levels to sustain koi metabolism. Some oxygen will diffuse directly into the water from air bubbles, but the main benefit of aeration systems is the churning effect they have on the surface, allowing oxygen to enter the water and carbon dioxide to dissipate. You can introduce air in the following ways.

Surface skimmer

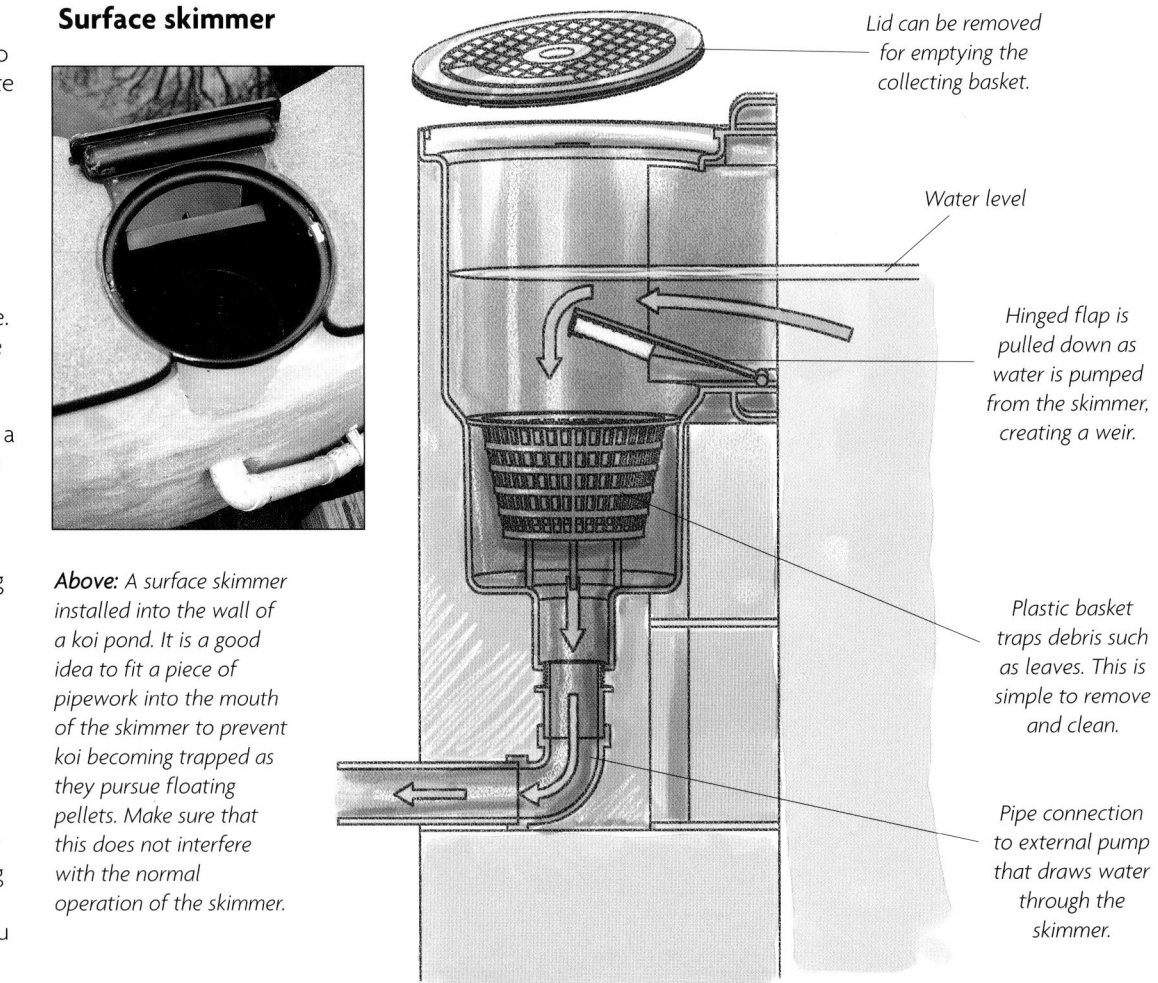

Above: *A surface skimmer installed into the wall of a koi pond. It is a good idea to fit a piece of pipework into the mouth of the skimmer to prevent koi becoming trapped as they pursue floating pellets. Make sure that this does not interfere with the normal operation of the skimmer.*

Lid can be removed for emptying the collecting basket.

Water level

Hinged flap is pulled down as water is pumped from the skimmer, creating a weir.

Plastic basket traps debris such as leaves. This is simple to remove and clean.

Pipe connection to external pump that draws water through the skimmer.

How a venturi works

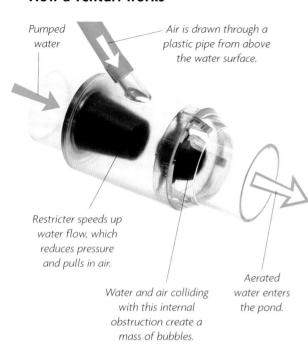

Pumped water

Air is drawn through a plastic pipe from above the water surface.

Restricter speeds up water flow, which reduces pressure and pulls in air.

Water and air colliding with this internal obstruction create a mass of bubbles.

Aerated water enters the pond.

Using a venturi This simple device fitted in the pumped return pipe underwater draws in air from above the surface and mixes it with the water passing through to create millions of tiny bubbles. Venturis need a strong water pressure to work efficiently and are not suitable for all types of pumps. Once a familiar sight in koi ponds, venturis are now proving less popular. One reason for this is that the new low-wattage, low-running-cost pumps do not deliver sufficient water pressure. Also, reliable airpumps are now reasonably priced and are the best way to aerate your koi pond.

Using an airpump This is the best way to aerate your pond. You can feed the pumped air into the water in two ways, through an aerator dome or via airstones.

An aerator dome is a special type of bottom drain used in gravity-fed ponds. An airline from the pump is fed into the drain and the air is released as a column of rising bubbles from a perforated membrane across the top of the dome. Depending on the type of aerator dome you choose, you will need to decide at the building stage whether to install it because you will need to concrete extra pipework into the base of the pond.

Airstones provide the most flexible way of getting air into the pond. They are available in a range of shapes and sizes, the ceramic ones being particularly good at producing a fine stream of bubbles. The simplest way of using an airstone is to connect it to the airpump with plastic airline and drop it over the side of the pond where you need it. You can also use airstones in filter systems to boost the oxygen levels for aerobic bacteria.

Above: This is the type of airpump used to aerate water in a koi system, either in the pond or in the filter chambers. These pumps need to be robust and powerful to supply a useful number of airstones.

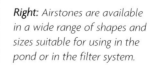

Left: The mass of bubbles arising from an airstone not only help oxygen to enter the water directly, but also create surface turbulence that aids gaseous exchange.

Right: Airstones are available in a wide range of shapes and sizes suitable for using in the pond or in the filter system.

Ozone unit

Inlet for ozone mixing with incoming water.

Valve to control water flow.

Connection to carbon filter to remove excess ozone and prevent it being released into the air.

Gravity return to pond.

UV unit burns off excess ozone in water.

Probe from redox meter inserted here measures ozone levels in the water and controls dosing rate.

Water pumped in from last filter chamber.

Ozone generator

Discharge to waste

Ozone gas reacts with pond water in this chamber.

Ozone systems

Using ozone is an accepted and familiar technique in the aquarium hobby – particularly in tropical marine fish tanks – but its use in koi ponds is a relatively new application. Ozone (O_3) is an unstable form of oxygen (O_2) and is generated by passing air through a high-voltage electrical discharge. The extra atom of oxygen attached to each molecule easily detaches and in the process has a powerful disinfectant effect, killing any living organisms or cells in the water close by.

Right: Colourful, healthy koi swimming in crystal clear water is the dream of all koi-keepers. Treating the water with the highly reactive gas ozone can help to keep the water free of disease bacteria and parasites, as well as helping to improve its overall clarity.

Clearly, it is also dangerous to the koi and it is vital that no ozone reaches the pond itself.

Pond water is pumped into the ozone unit, either by the main pump or a separate one, and the flow rate through it depends on the pond volume and the size of the unit. Once treated, the water returns to the pond by gravity.

An ozone unit has a marked beneficial effect on koi welfare because it is effectively a self-contained water treatment plant. It will reduce levels of harmful bacteria and parasites, improve water clarity and reduce health problems in the long term. Unfortunately, ozone systems are very expensive and thus out of the reach of many koi-keepers. They can be added later and so are worth considering if your budget allows.

Protein skimmer

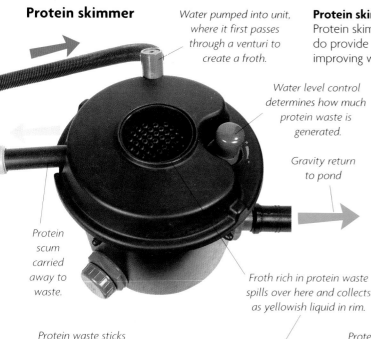

Water pumped into unit, where it first passes through a venturi to create a froth.

Water level control determines how much protein waste is generated.

Gravity return to pond

Protein scum carried away to waste.

Froth rich in protein waste spills over here and collects as yellowish liquid in rim.

Protein waste sticks to air bubbles and is carried upwards into the top of the unit.

Protein scum carried away to waste.

Air is added to the incoming water flow to generate a froth. In suitable units, ozone can be added at this stage.

Cleaned water returns to the pond by gravity.

Protein skimmers

Protein skimmers are not essential items but they do provide a way of reducing surface foam and improving water clarity. They make use of the natural tendency for organic molecules to stick to the surface of bubbles. The organic molecules in a koi pond are the fatty and protein waste materials produced by the fish. (The same process is at work in a washing machine as the 'dirt' is 'lifted' off the clothes into the cleansing foam.) The bubbles are created in a protein skimmer by pumping the incoming water through a venturi (see page 29) and keeping them in contact with the water for as long as possible before it returns to the pond by gravity. The air bubbles become coated in protein waste and rise to a collecting cup at the top of the unit. As the bubbles burst, they release the waste and the yellow liquid that builds up can be drained off and discarded. To combine the cleaning and disinfectant process, ozone can be introduced into the airflow at the venturi stage.

Installing a UV clarifier

Although not essential, a UV clarifier will help to keep the water clear by specifically controlling green water – a suspension of single-celled algae boosted by sunlight and high levels of fertilisers such as nitrates and phosphates. Inside the unit a fluorescent tube radiates ultraviolet (UV) – short wavelength light at the far end of the purple region of the visible

UV clarifier

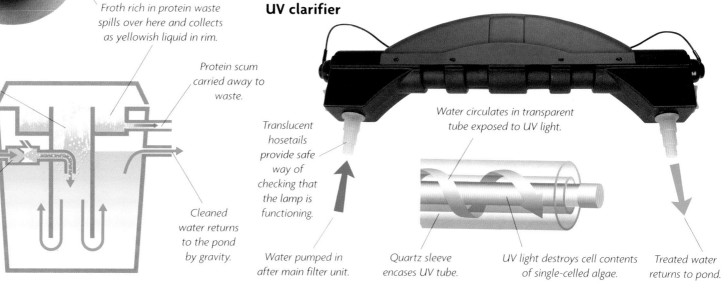

Translucent hosetails provide safe way of checking that the lamp is functioning.

Water circulates in transparent tube exposed to UV light.

Water pumped in after main filter unit.

Quartz sleeve encases UV tube.

UV light destroys cell contents of single-celled algae.

Treated water returns to pond.

spectrum. UV light is harmful to living tissue and at the right concentration will disrupt the cell contents of the algae, causing them to collapse and decay.

It is important here to make a distinction between a UV clarifier used on a pond and a UV steriliser more commonly used in the tropical freshwater and marine aquarium hobbies. The clarifier allows a relatively large volume of water to pass over the UV light, whereas a steriliser allows a small volume of water to flow close to the light so that it receives a higher 'dose'. This means that a clarifier will affect just the green algae cells, while a steriliser – which has a higher light output as well – is designed to control some bacteria and parasites in the water.

For a UV clarifier to be effective, it is vital to match the power of the unit to the pond volume. As a general rule, allow 10 watts of UV light power per 4,500 litres (1,000 gallons) of pond volume. Clarifiers are available in power ratings from 6 to 55 watts, so the largest of these would be ideal for a pond of 25,000 litres (5,500 gallons). For bigger ponds, use multiple units to reach the target level and always aim on the generous side. The other important factor is the speed of water through the clarifier. To operate efficiently, the UV light should treat the whole pond volume once every two hours. If the flow is too fast, the algae cells will not receive sufficient UV light to be affected. If the flow is too slow, algal growth will outstrip the treatment rate. Always fit the clarifier in the system where it will directly receive pumped water.

Regular maintenance is a must. Clean the quartz sleeve housing the tube regularly, but do take care because the sleeve is extremely fragile. Replace the UV tube every 6-12 months, because the useful light output will have fallen dramatically. Fit your clarifier in a position that allows you sufficient space to slide the fluorescent tube out – a larger unit will need up to 1m (39in) clearance. Despite popular misconceptions, a UV clarifier will not have any effect on blanketweed, the thick grasslike algae that grows from the sides and base of the pond. Several strategies are effective against blanketweed, including electronic controllers (see page 33 for more details).

Fluidised sand bed filters
These offer the benefits of biological filtration in a very compact unit. Pond water is pumped into a chamber containing a small quantity of special silica sand. The sand swirls up into a constantly moving suspension and the beneficial bacteria that thrive on the surface of the grains cleanse the water of biological wastes. As with ozone units and protein skimmers, the treated water returns to the pond by gravity.

Water polishing units
Water polishing is literally the process of producing 'crystal clear' water in the pond. The traditional way of doing this has been to install a sand filter after the last main filter stage and just before the water returns to the pond. Sand filters – typically used in swimming pool treatment plants – need a high-pressure, power-hungry pump to force water through fine sand in a sealed container. They provide no biological filtration effect but certainly improve water clarity, albeit with a high-maintenance tariff.

Sand filters for koi pond use are being superseded by technically less demanding and more cost-effective water polishing units. These take many

Fluidised bed filter

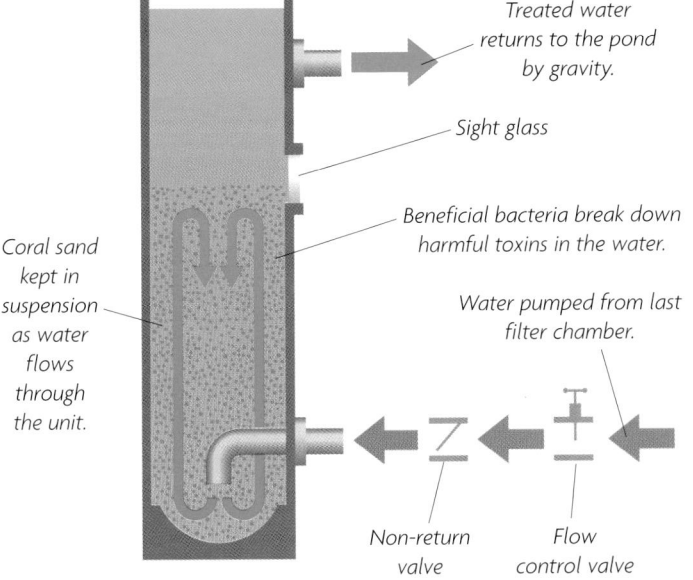

Treated water returns to the pond by gravity.

Sight glass

Beneficial bacteria break down harmful toxins in the water.

Water pumped from last filter chamber.

Coral sand kept in suspension as water flows through the unit.

Non-return valve

Flow control valve

Sieve plate filter

Water pumped from last filter chamber.

Filter body contains core of sieve plates.

Core of overlapping sieve plates.

Drain port for dirt and trapped debris.

'Polished' water returns to the pond by gravity.

forms, but generally consist of a canister containing a sieve or series of sieve plates that trap very small particles. Although they do not need the high-pressure pump used for a sand filter, they do require a certain amount of pressure to work efficiently. Regular cleaning of the sieve plates is paramount, particularly when first installed.

Electronic blanketweed devices

Strands of green algae – known as blanketweed – that commonly grow in all kinds of ponds not only look unsightly and cause lowered oxygen levels in summer,

Above: The plastic sieve plates can be removed from the stack for cleaning. Different grades of plates are available.

Right: A close-up of the sieve plates reveals fine ridges on the overlapping surfaces that trap debris from the water flow.

Electronic blanketweed controller

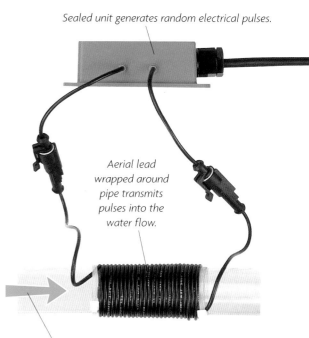

Sealed unit generates random electrical pulses.

Aerial lead wrapped around pipe transmits pulses into the water flow.

Water pumped from last filter chamber.

but also clog filters, drains, pumps and pipework. Various strategies exist to discourage and clear blanketweed, including chemicals, barley straw and electronic devices that disrupt the algal cells by pulsing magnetic and radio waves through them. Electronic units are easy to install and seem to have the greatest deterrent effect when added to a new pond that has never suffered blanketweed problems.

A fascination with koi can begin at an early age, leading to the next generation of koi pond builders.

Part Two

Building your koi pond

In this section, we look at the two most popular methods of making a koi pond: using a liner or constructing a block-built shell that is then rendered and fibreglassed. We examine each method, from the initial excavation right through to filling and adding the finishing touches to the pond, such as laying decking and edging.

Although the ideal method of construction is to block-build and fibreglass, this is not always the best strategy or possible. If that is the case, it is better to acknowledge it early on and opt for an alternative construction method that suits your needs and ability. Building a koi pond can be technically demanding and it is important that it is done correctly, as the finished pond will be under a lot of stress from the water pressure. This section is not intended to give you a crash course in building techniques; rather, it is designed to illustrate and explain each stage involved in the construction process. Unless you are comfortable about laying concrete, building walls, rendering, etc., it is best to seek professional help and advice. This can take one of two forms. The first is to employ a specialist pond building company to build the whole pond. Alternatively, if you understand the principles involved, you can employ skilled tradespeople to carry out each task. If you opt for this method, it will be your responsibility to ensure that they are on site at the correct time, that all the machinery can gain access and to arrange suitable insurance for any machinery used. In effect, it means that you become the foreman for the whole project.

So read this part of the book and if the prospect of building the pond yourself leaves you feeling daunted by the whole idea, the best course is probably to bring in the professionals. Even if you are confident that you can carry out the work yourself, it is still a good idea to run through your plans with your local koi dealer to make sure they are feasible. No matter how well planned, there is always one detail that is overlooked and it is far better to have potential problems pointed out at an early stage than to discover them halfway through the project when it is too late to put them right.

Liner pond – estimating the size

A liner pond is by far the easiest form of pond to install and suitable not only as a garden pond but also, despite popular belief, for koi. A liner pond is thought to be inappropriate for koi because if it is to include a gravity-fed filtration system, it means making holes in the liner for drains and returns, thereby risking leakages. However, it is not difficult to install these pieces of equipment, although you must take extra care when carrying out the work. If you follow the steps outlined here, you should have no problem setting up a well-functioning, watertight, gravity-fed pond using a liner.

Many people find the prospect of installing a liner pond less daunting than building a block-built one because the construction process simply involves

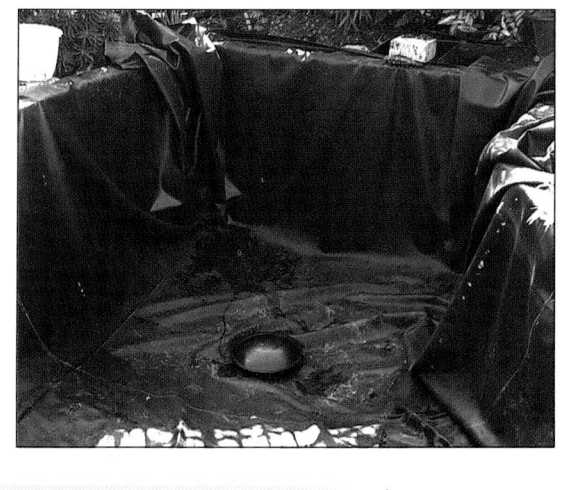

digging a hole and putting in the liner. This is certainly true, although obviously adding a gravity-fed filter system requires a certain amount of extra construction to ensure that the drains do not move about. This normally means encasing the pipework in a channel of concrete. There is no need to construct a solid base or 23cm (9in) block walls up from the base, as the overall strength of the pond is provided by the liner and the soil behind it. (On the other hand, the resilience of a block-built pond depends on the quality of the overall construction.)

The only other construction work involves laying a concrete collar around the top of the pond for support, plus any above-ground brickwork if the pond is to be raised above ground level. If this is the case, follow the construction techniques described on pages 46-59. We will now examine all the other aspects involved in building a liner pond.

Raised ponds

If you are planning to raise a liner pond out of the ground, build the walls using 23cm (9in) reinforced hollow concrete blocks. Tie these to the concrete collar around the rim of the pond using reinforced steel rods. You can then face them with brickwork, as shown in this pond.

Above: *A liner pond is literally a hole in the ground lined with a rubber or plastic sheet to stop the water draining away. The most important thing is to make sure the liner is big enough.*

What you will need

Concrete	Underlay
Ballast	Cold glue tape
Sand	Edging slabs or rocks
110mm (4in) bottom drain	Digger or shovel
110mm (4in) pipe for drain	Skips or grabber lorries
38 or 50mm (1.5-2in) pipe	to remove waste
for return pipework	Insurance for any
Filter	machinery on site, such
Pump	as diggers or hired tools
UV clarifier	Blocks if the pond is to
Liner	be built above ground
	Mortar for blocks

Working out the size of the liner

To work out the size of the liner you need for your pond, first measure the length, width and depth of your excavation. Then double the depth measurement and add this figure to both the length and the width measurements. You will also need to allow for an overlap around the edge so that you can anchor and conceal the liner with stones, bricks or slabs. Adding 60cm (24in) to the adjusted length and width measurements will give you a 30cm (12in) overlap around the perimeter.

Depth

Length

Width

Polyester underlay. Use this to protect the liner from any sharp stones underneath it.

PVC liner 0.5mm (0.02in) thick. Suitable for watercourses and small ponds.

Composite liner 0.55mm (0.022in) thick. Thermoplastic elastomer layered with reinforcing mesh.

Butyl rubber 0.75mm (0.03in) thick. Long-lasting liner that can be welded.

EPDM rubber 1.0mm (0.04in) thick. Heavyweight liner with good strength and durability, although it may prove difficult to mould into shape.

Overlap margin of 30cm (12in) around the edge.

Right: Good-quality liner is heavy and difficult to handle on your own. You will need help to move a large liner into place.

Liner pond – making a concrete collar

To create a firm and even foundation for the liner and edging stones and to prevent the soil collapsing as you dig the hole, first build a concrete collar (also called a ring beam) around the pond edge. Building the collar before digging the pond means that the soil on either side will act as shuttering, which helps to create a suitable structure and reduces the work involved. Plan where the returns and pipework are to go and incorporate them into the collar.

Once the concrete collar has set, begin digging out the pond. If you are opting for a gravity-fed system (see page 14), try to dig out a slight gradient running from the outside walls to the centre or to the point where you intend placing the bottom drain. Also dig out the site for the filter, allowing for the fact that when the excavation is complete, the top of the filter should be about 2.5cm (1in) above the water level in the pond.

When the initial excavation is complete, and if you are installing a bottom drain, dig the trench for the pipework. This trench will be used to run the 110mm (4in) pipe from the drain to the pond, and will be filled with concrete to keep everything in place. Due to the weight that will be placed on the drain and pipe, it is essential that they are laid onto a concrete base, so make the trench 38cm (15in) deep and as wide as possible. Eventually, the drain and pipe should be surrounded by at least 15cm (6in) of concrete. Once the trench is dug, pour in an initial layer of concrete at least 15cm (6in) deep. When it has set, lay out the drain and pipework and pour in the second base of concrete to hold everything securely in position.

Start by marking out the internal shape of the pond with pegs and string. When you are happy with the shape, set out a second series of pegs 23cm (9in) away from the first, mirroring the internal shape.

Dig out a trench 23cm (9in) deep between the two series of pegs. If the ground is uneven, remove the two sets of marker pegs and reposition them vertically along the centre of the trench. Check that the tops of the pegs are level all the way round and adjust any that are not.

Be sure to position surface skimmers and pipework before pouring concrete into the trench.

The concrete collar will provide a level base for the edging stones and will be disguised by them.

Once you have laid in any return pipework, etc., pour the concrete into the trench up to the top of each peg. Leave the pegs in place.

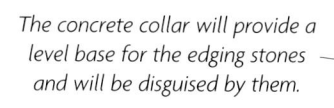

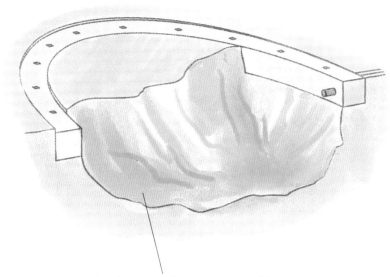

Dome   Flange

Drain casing

When the concrete has set, you can safely excavate the soil inside the collar. Make the base as flat as possible so that the liner will fit smoothly later on.

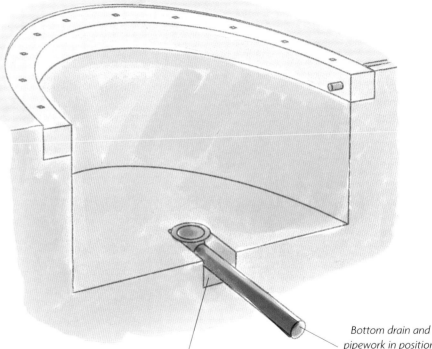

Left: If you are digging out the cavity with a spade, try not to stand on the collar as you dig and do not use it as a lever for the spade, otherwise the edge will break.

Mark out the position of the bottom drain and 110mm (4in) pipe run. These must be totally encased in concrete, so dig a trench in the base of the excavation about 38cm (15in) deep. Fill the trench with about 15cm (6in) of concrete to support the drain and pipe run and allow it to set.

Bottom drain and pipework in position, ready to be encased in concrete.

The pipe from the drain will run to the edge of the pond, where it will be extended up to ground level ready to be cut down for connection to the filter system. Encase this pipe in concrete as well, because it will be subjected to the sidewards pressure of the water in the pond.

When all the concrete has set, line the pond with underlay in preparation for the liner. A layer of sand beneath the underlay provides extra protection. Cut holes in the underlay around the bottom drains and any inlet pipe. Make absolutely sure that no underlay runs over any flanges that will be sealed to the liner at a later stage, otherwise it may not be possible to achieve a watertight seal.

Now place the liner into position, ready for sealing onto the bottom drain. Before cutting any holes, be sure to push the liner firmly into all the corners, so that it cannot move once it is sealed. If you wish, you can fill the pond with a small amount of water to ensure that the liner is secure. Then pump away the water and leave the liner to dry.

Box welding for liner ponds

You can order a liner made to fit your pond exactly, with no folds or creases. Your koi dealer will weld panels of liner together to match the excavation. This works best for formal-shaped ponds, such as circular, rectangular or square.

Right: *Before installing the underlay, sweep the concrete collar free of stones that could fall into the excavation. Also remove any stones in the hole and prise out roots from nearby trees. If you stood on a sharp stone during the installation, you could puncture the liner before you have even added water to the pond.*

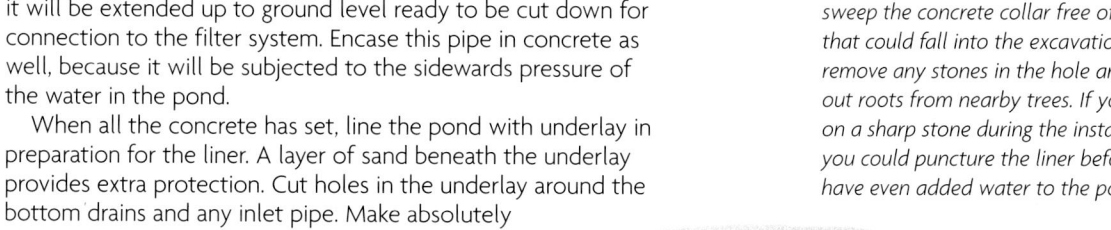

Pumped return pipe protruding through concrete collar.

Sand layer to cushion the underlay and liner.

Place the drain and pipework on top of the set concrete layer in the trench and encase them in concrete. Do not attach the domed cover of the bottom drain at this stage.

Left: Spun underlays are by far the best, as they allow water to move through them. This prevents water from being trapped between the liner and underlay and stops roots penetrating the liner. Buy more than you need so that you have some to spare for a waterfall if you plan to include one.

Below: When you get your pond liner home, check it carefully for tears and imperfections; once you have installed it, you will not be able to remove it. Replace the liner in its packaging and store it in a safe place until you are ready to use it.

You can get into the pond (without your shoes) to pleat and fold any creases. Use cold-glue tape to secure them if necessary.

Lay a 5cm (2in) layer of sand over the base, and line the excavation and collar with underlay. Offer the liner into position, taking care not to dislodge the underlay.

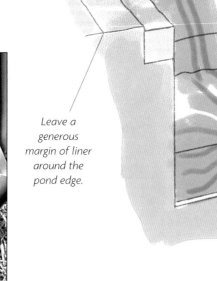

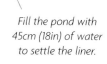

Leave a generous margin of liner around the pond edge.

Fill the pond with 45cm (18in) of water to settle the liner.

When you are satisfied that the liner is in place, locate the top flanges for the drain and other pipework in the correct position and secure them with a suitable sealer and the screws supplied with the fittings. Only now should you begin to make any incisions into the liner. When cutting holes it is best to work from the centre outwards, using the secured fittings as your cutting guide. If the holes are cut before the fittings are in position, it may prove impossible to match them up!

Place a pump in the bottom drain and pump away the water. Thoroughly dry the liner and connect the flange onto the bottom drain. Fit the dome cover and all tank connectors, in accordance with the manufacturer's instructions.

Before fitting the tank connector, secure it to the liner (i.e. on both sides of the liner with the stainless steel screws screwed up) using a suitable sealant. Then cut through the liner to make the hole. If you make the hole before securing the tank connector, the cut edges do not lie flat and it is difficult to get a smooth union. Solvent-weld the tank connector to the return pipe in the wall of the pond.

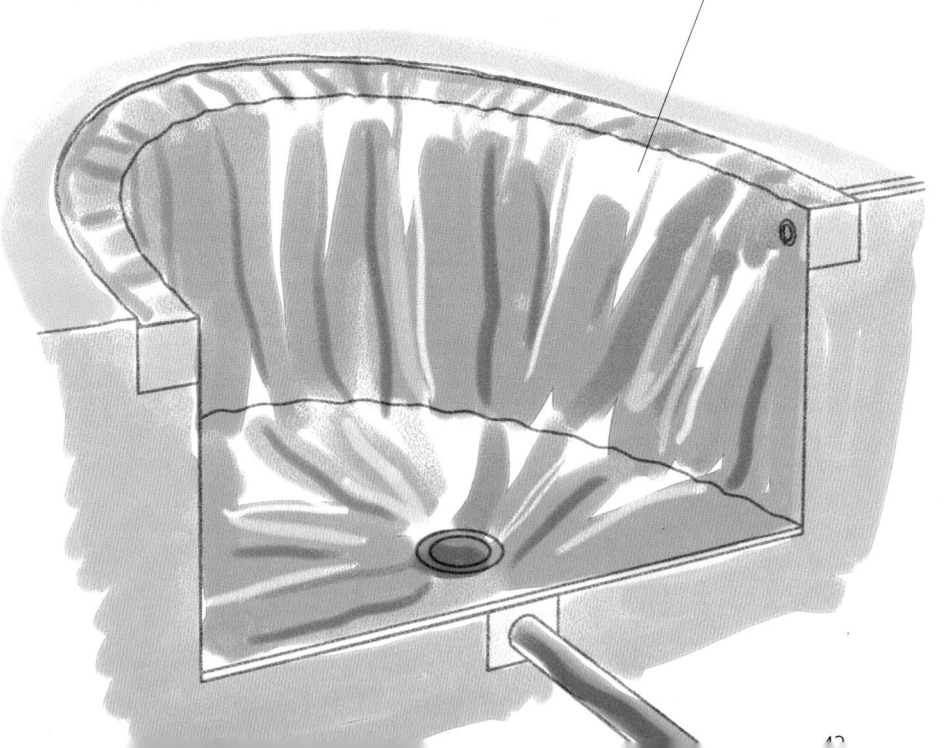

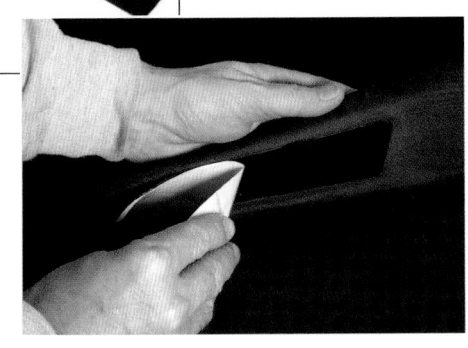

Left: *The best way of minimising creases in a pond liner is to use cold glue tape, which is like a heavy duty version of double-sided tape.*

Right: *Warm the tape first with a hairdryer and stick it to the edge of the fold. Remove the paper backing and push the fold in place. It will be hard to re-position once fixed.*

Securing the bottom drain

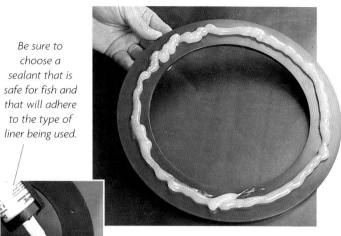

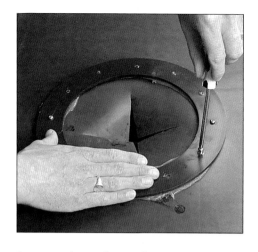

Be sure to choose a sealant that is safe for fish and that will adhere to the type of liner being used.

1 When the liner is fully in place, climb into the pond and locate the drain through the liner. Place the top flange in position and hold it steady as you make a small incision in the liner inside the flange.

2 Take the flange and cover the underside with a suitable sealant ready for sealing in place. Do not hold back on the sealant as this will create the watertight seal.

3 Position the top flange, which is covered in sealant, onto the liner so that it lines up with the base of the drain. Once aligned, tighten the screws to secure the unit.

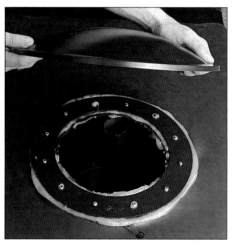

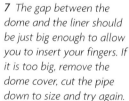

4 Using a knife, extend your initial incision in the liner outwards to the now fully secured flange. Trim away the unwanted liner, following the circumference of the flange with your knife.

5 The pipe that fits into the drain allows you to set the dome height. Push it into the socket on the bottom of the unit, but do not glue it in place as you may need to remove it for access at a later date.

6 With the pipe in place, push the dome cover onto it. Again, do not glue in position in case you need to remove it in the future.

7 The gap between the dome and the liner should be just big enough to allow you to insert your fingers. If it is too big, remove the dome cover, cut the pipe down to size and try again.

Liner pond – the finishing touches

The pond is now ready to fill. However, one thing you may wish to do before filling the pond is secure any creases in the liner using a product called 'cold glue tape'. This double-sided tape is normally 5cm (2in) wide and supplied in 1m (39in) or 10m (33ft) rolls. To be effective, the liner must be dry and clean before you apply any tape. It also helps to warm the tape with a hairdryer before use. To determine where any creases may occur, add a small amount of water to the pond to pull the sides of the liner tight as shown on page 41. Then empty the pond again and let the liner dry out before applying the tape.

To finish off the final edging around the pond, use coping stones, rock, bricks or any another suitable material. There are various ways of neatening the edges of the liner, but do not forget that it is creating a waterproof seal and must therefore run under or up whatever edging you choose.

Your liner pond is now complete and all that remains is to install the filters, which must be level with the water in the pond. The installation of the filter system is explained on pages 46-59 for a block-built pond, but the same method applies here. When it is in place and all the pipework is connected, fill the pond and commission the system.

Left: A typical water meter, with connections to fit a standard hosepipe. These units do not normally reset to zero, so it is important to note the start reading before using the meter so that you can subtract it from the final reading.

Complete the edge of the pond with slabs, brickwork, slate or stones and fill the pond using a flowmeter.

Use a tank connector to seal the liner to the pipe. Make a watertight seal, using a suitable sealant, as explained on page 42. Cut the return pipe flush with the liner.

Above: *The paving slabs used along the edge of this liner pond have lost their new 'rawness' and have taken on a more mellow, aged appearance. They provide a stable platform for fish viewing.*

Alternative pond edgings

Left: *You can conceal the edge of the liner between vertical courses of bricks, as shown here. The concrete collar makes an ideal foundation for the brickwork. If the pond is to be raised by more than a few courses, build it up with blocks and finish the external walls with brick, concealing the liner between the blocks and brickwork.*

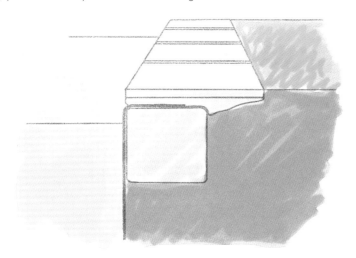

Left: *Slabs form a neat and stable edge for a koi pond. The underlay and liner overlap the concrete collar and are covered by paving.*

Right: *If you place boulders around the edge, support them on a liner offcut to protect the pond liner.*

Block-built pond – planning and excavation

In this part of the book, we are following the steps involved in the construction of a partly raised, oval, concrete-rendered koi pond. It will have an estimated capacity of 22,700 litres (5,000 gallons) and be equipped with a vortex filtration system, heating, UV clarifier, aeration and a water purifier.

Start by marking out the area on the ground. This pond will measure approximately 4.5x3m (15x10ft), but an extra 35cm (14in) has been allowed all the way round to incorporate a 23cm (9in) block wall, part of which will have a brickwork facing. As the pond is to be 60cm (24in) above ground level, excavate the area to a depth of 135cm (54in) so that the final pond depth will be approximately 1.5m (5ft).

Having completed the pond excavation, set out the area for the filter system. In this instance it will require a floor area of 3.7x2.5m (12x8ft) and will be the same depth as the pond. To determine the exact height needed for the filters, adjust the thickness of the concrete base laid in this area.

This is also a good time to think about the pipework that will return the water to the pond, plus any additional pipework that may be needed for removing waste water. Consider where it will go and, if necessary, excavate the designated areas. If the pond is some distance from utilities such as water and electricity, you could run a trench for them now, as this may be the only time when an excavator is on site.

How to mark out a shape

Marking out the shape of your new pond on the ground and trying to get an idea of how it will look in your garden are vital first steps in the planning process. The small-scale examples in these photographs demonstrate some simple techniques for marking our circles and ovals. Instead of sand in a bottle, you could use a can of spray chalk.

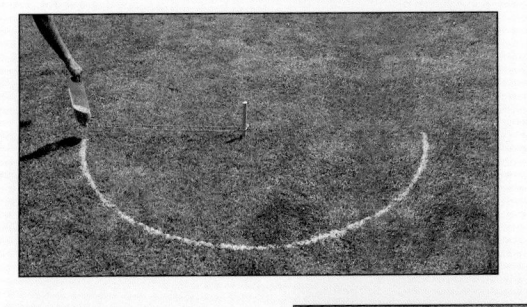

Left: *To mark out a circle, position your marker inside a loop of string held taut around a peg at the centre of the space.*

Right: *Using a loop of string running around two pegs spaced apart will give you a perfect oval shape on the ground.*

Left: *For informal shapes, lay a brightly coloured hosepipe on the ground and view the results from an upstairs window until you are happy with the result.*

The pond construction

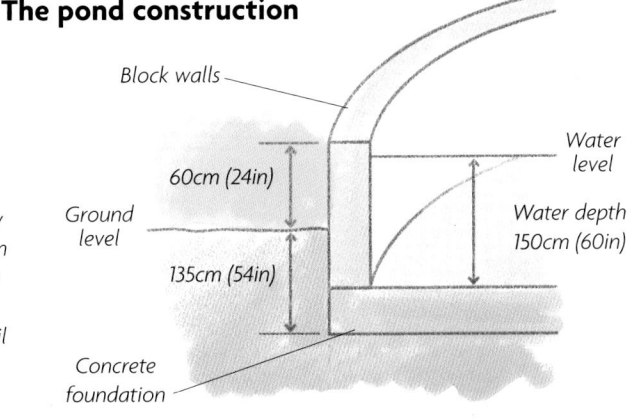

Block walls

Water level

Ground level

60cm (24in)

Water depth 150cm (60in)

135cm (54in)

Concrete foundation

Water level in the pond and filter

The water level in the pond determines the height of the filter system. The level must be the same in each for the gravity-fed system to work.

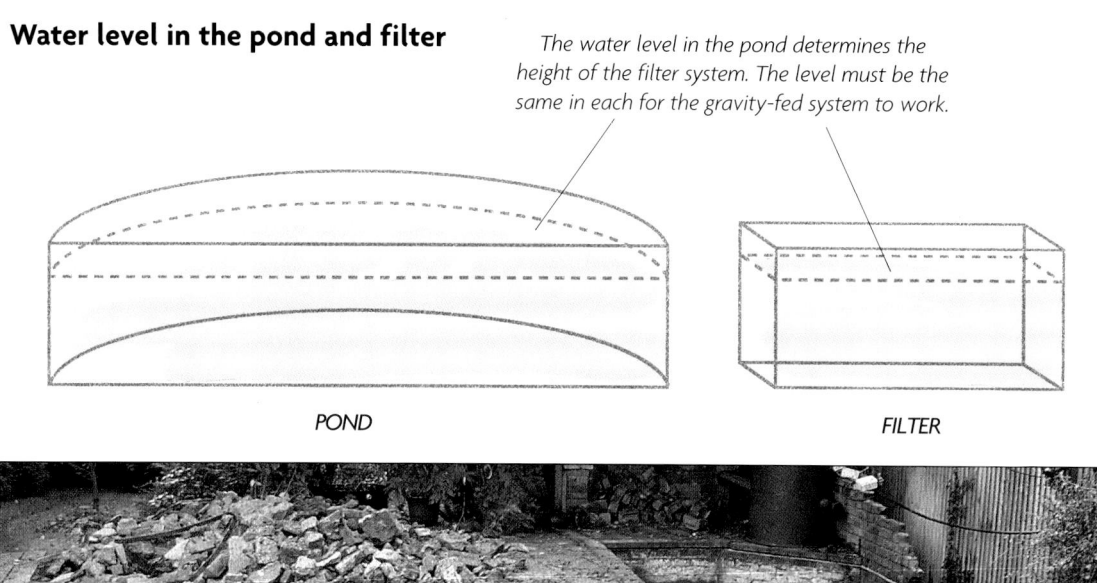

POND   FILTER

Above: A mini digger in action. These machines can be hired with or without a driver, and are invaluable if there is access to the site. Remember that while the machine is on hire it is your responsibility, so take out insurance against theft or damage.

Right: The excavated pond and filter chamber, ready for the concrete base to be laid. The backwash pipe leading from an existing swimming pool discovered in the centre of the excavation was covered in a steel plate and concreted over before the main foundation was laid.

Block-built pond – laying the foundations

Now it is time to construct the base of the pond by pouring in concrete to a final depth of 30-45cm (12-18in). When you have added the first 15-20cm (6-8in) of concrete, allow it to set. Then lay in the 12-18mm (0.5-0.75in)-gauge reinforced steel bars and position the bottom drain, or drains. Add more concrete until you reach the final depth and allow the finished base to set. Do not pour the concrete base into the filter area at this stage, as it is vital that the water level of the pond and that of the vortex system are the same. You will not be able to judge this until the walls of the pond are built.

Right: An alternative method of construction involves laying a matrix of reinforced steel before any concrete is poured. It is raised off the ground with blocks, so that the concrete flows around the steel, creating a single cast base with the reinforcements in it. Notice that the bottom drain in the middle, (which is a different design from the one featured elsewhere in this book), is covered to prevent any cement falling into it as the concrete base is poured.

Constructing a large koi pond

This large project incorporates a number of bottom drains. A concrete base is laid first and allowed to set. This technique means that the drains can be laid and checked for levels, and all the pipework put in position before the next layer of concrete is poured.

Left: A layer of steel reinforcement is laid on top of the first slab of concrete, then the second batch of concrete is laid and levelled as it is poured. During this process it is a good idea to fill all the drain pipework with water to weight it down and prevent it floating in the concrete.

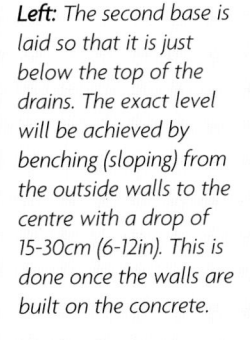

Left: The second base is laid so that it is just below the top of the drains. The exact level will be achieved by benching (sloping) from the outside walls to the centre with a drop of 15-30cm (6-12in). This is done once the walls are built on the concrete.

Using an aerated bottom drain

If your pond design incorporates an aerated bottom drain, it may be necessary to run additional pipework in the base of the pond to accommodate the airline that delivers the air to the unit. This type of bottom drain cannot be added at a later stage, so you must decide early in the construction process whether you want to use one in the pond.

Installing the bottom drain

Push – never glue – a drain cover into place, leaving a gap of 13-25mm (0.5-1in).

The 110mm (4in) pipe to the filter must be as level as possible to avoid waste collecting in any high or low points.

A second layer of concrete encases all the pipework and drains.

Concrete sub-base

Steel reinforcing mesh

Laying the foundations

A 110mm (4in) pipe runs from the bottom drain to the filter system.

The walls of the pond are built onto a concrete base, The thicker the base the better, as each 1000 litres (220 gallons) of water weighs about 990kg (2200lb).

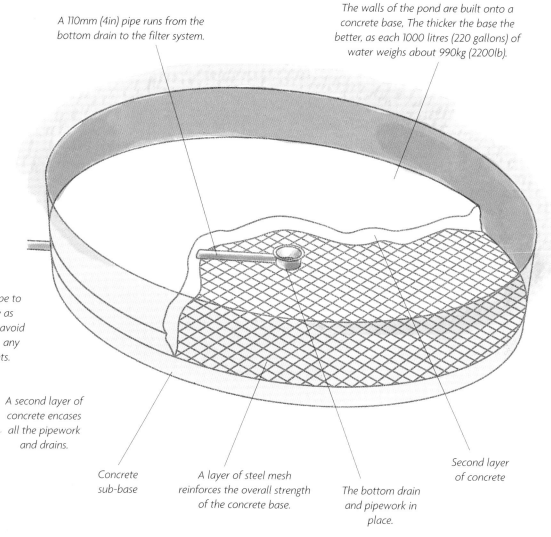

Concrete sub-base

A layer of steel mesh reinforces the overall strength of the concrete base.

The bottom drain and pipework in place.

Second layer of concrete

Block-built pond – building the walls

Build up the pond walls using 23cm (9in) reinforced hollow blocks. These create a honeycomb effect and must be backfilled with concrete. At the same time, insert 16-20mm (0.625-0.8in)-gauge reinforced steel bars. As you build up the blockwork, allow for two water returns leading from the pond to the filter system. One return should be 30-35cm (12-14in) below the water surface and the other 30-35cm (12-14in) up from the base of the pond. These returns should pass through the wall of the pond at an angle of 45°, so that optimum water circulation can be achieved within the pond. This type of return is known as a TPR (Tangential Pond Return). As you complete the last course of blocks, set the surface skimmer at the 'end' of the water's circulation around the pond to ensure that all surface debris is pushed towards the skimmer. Depending on the type of skimmer, the water level may not be at the top of the unit. Position the skimmer so that when the pond is filled, the water is at the correct level. When the pond is the required height, and while you wait for the blockwork to dry, you can install the filter system.

Above: The pond walls are built from 23cm (9in) hollow blocks. The finish is somewhat untidy, but eventually both sides will be rendered. Alternatively, the external walls can be hidden behind face brickwork.

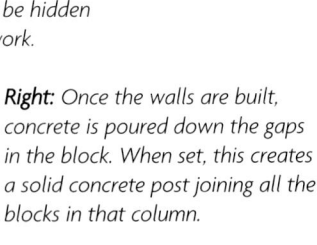

Right: Once the walls are built, concrete is poured down the gaps in the block. When set, this creates a solid concrete post joining all the blocks in that column.

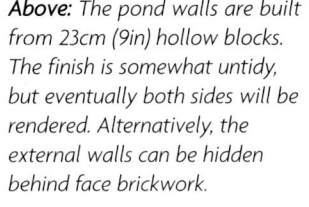

Adding extra strength

Reinforced steel bars add strength to block walls. The more you use, the stronger the construction. As a guide, use vertical bars at any weak points, such as the corners on a square pond, or at strategic points on a curved or circular pond.

Below: *This construction uses the highest level of reinforcement, with vertical steel bars placed in all the blocks and horizontal ones laid between each course of blockwork.*

The walls take shape

Position the surface skimmer in the block wall where the water flow generated by the pumped returns will 'push' floating debris towards it.

Outlet from skimmer to external pump

Pumped return from filter

Water circulates around pond towards the skimmer.

The pumped returns from the filter enter the pond at an angle of approximately 45° to generate an optimum water flow around the pond.

The pond walls are constructed using 23x45cm (9x18in) hollow concrete blocks, which are then backfilled with concrete.

Bottom drain encased in concrete. The dome will be fitted later on.

Installing the surface skimmer

Left: Leave space in the wall of the pond for the surface skimmer. You can then position it before concreting it into place. Leave enough pipe on the feed from the skimmer so that you can cut it to the exact length once the skimmer is firmly set in place.

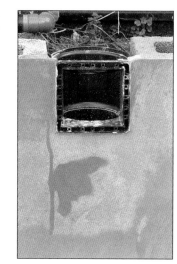

Left: A front view of the surface skimmer, with the render going up to the edge of the unit. Bear in mind that the final water level will be about halfway up the mouth of the skimmer.

How the filter connects with the pond

Before you fill the base of the filter with concrete, make sure that the tops of your filters are about 2.5cm (1in) above the intended water level in the pond. Use a laser level to help you arrive at the precise height of the filter system.

This pond system features three vortex chambers installed in a line. Connect vortex 1 to the bottom drain of the pond, with a 110mm (4in) slide valve fitted in line. Connect vortex 1, 2 and 3 using 110mm (4in) pipework and join vortex 3 to the pump using 38mm (1.5in) pipework. Before the pipe enters the pump, fit a T piece to allow the skimmer to be inserted into the pipe run. Water from the filter will flow into one side of the T piece and water from the skimmer into the other. Connect the 'combined' part of the T to the suction side of the pump. It is advisable to install a ball valve on all sides of the T to allow you to control the amount of water being drawn from the skimmer and filter independently.

On the flow side of the pump, the pipework should run to the UV unit and from there to a gas or electric heater. The flow from the heater will be divided between the two returns already built into the pond wall.

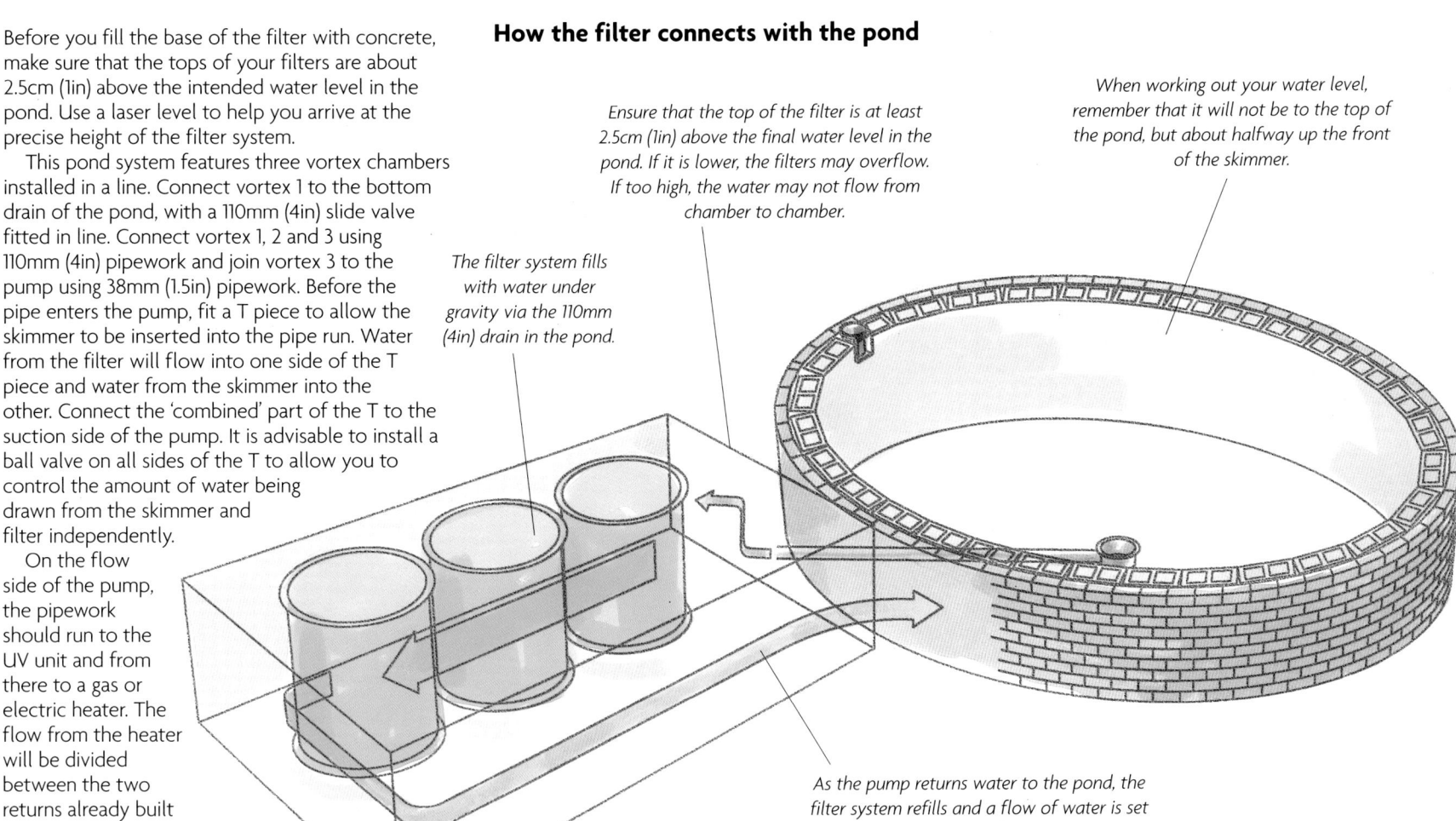

Ensure that the top of the filter is at least 2.5cm (1in) above the final water level in the pond. If it is lower, the filters may overflow. If too high, the water may not flow from chamber to chamber.

When working out your water level, remember that it will not be to the top of the pond, but about halfway up the front of the skimmer.

The filter system fills with water under gravity via the 110mm (4in) drain in the pond.

As the pump returns water to the pond, the filter system refills and a flow of water is set up through the unit.

How the filter system works

Slide valves ⊣⊢   Ball valves ⊙

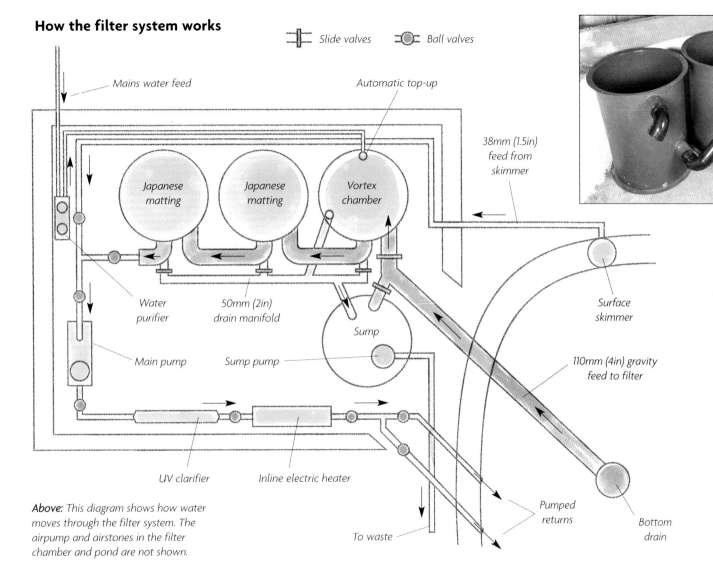

Mains water feed

Automatic top-up

38mm (1.5in) feed from skimmer

Japanese matting

Japanese matting

Vortex chamber

Water purifier

50mm (2in) drain manifold

Surface skimmer

Sump

Main pump

Sump pump

110mm (4in) gravity feed to filter

UV clarifier

Inline electric heater

Pumped returns

To waste

Bottom drain

Above: This diagram shows how water moves through the filter system. The airpump and airstones in the filter chamber and pond are not shown.

Above: When installing your filters, always do a dry run first. Position everything and make sure that all the pipework meets up before gluing them together. Here the pipe from the 110mm (4in) drain protrudes through the floor and has been left high, until the exact location of the filters is decided. Only then will it be cut down to the exact height. You can also see the drain points on the filters (two with valves fitted), and these will be plumbed in when all the other pipework is in place. A slide valve is installed on the inlet to the first vortex chamber. This allows for the filter system to be isolated from the pond and is especially useful for purging (flushing) the pipework from the drains.

To simplify any future maintenance of the filter system, you should fit 38mm (1.5in) ball valves on each side of the UV clarifier, heater, pump, skimmer and the two pond returns. This will enable you to remove and replace each piece of equipment individually.

Finally, fit the airstones from your chosen air system, the water purifying unit and a self-topping ballcock to vortex 1. If you decide to fit an overflow to the system, this should also be connected to vortex 1. Excavate a soakaway so that you can discharge the water from the vortex system for cleaning, and drain it away using a sump pump. The soakaway should be at least 5m (16ft) away from the house.

Small soakaway 75cm (30in) across and 105cm (42in) deep with a sump pump in the bottom, pumping to the main soakaway.

This overflow pipe from vortex 1 connects with a manifold of 50mm (2in) pipes connecting all three vortex chambers and carrying waste to the sump via 50mm (2in) slide valves.

These are the 110mm (4in) pipes connecting the three vortex chambers, from the top of one to the bottom of the next.

This is the 110mm (4in) feed from the bottom drain to the first vortex chamber.

This 82mm (3in) pipe and valve enables the bottom drain to be flushed without interfering with the vortex chambers.

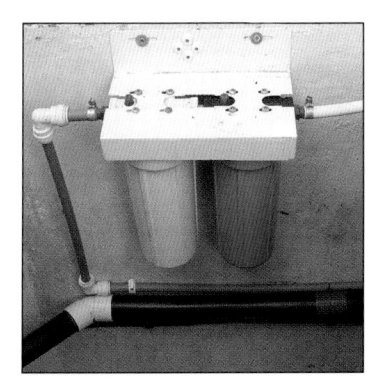

Right: The water purifier is fed with mains water and supplies treated water to the self-topping ballcock in the first vortex.

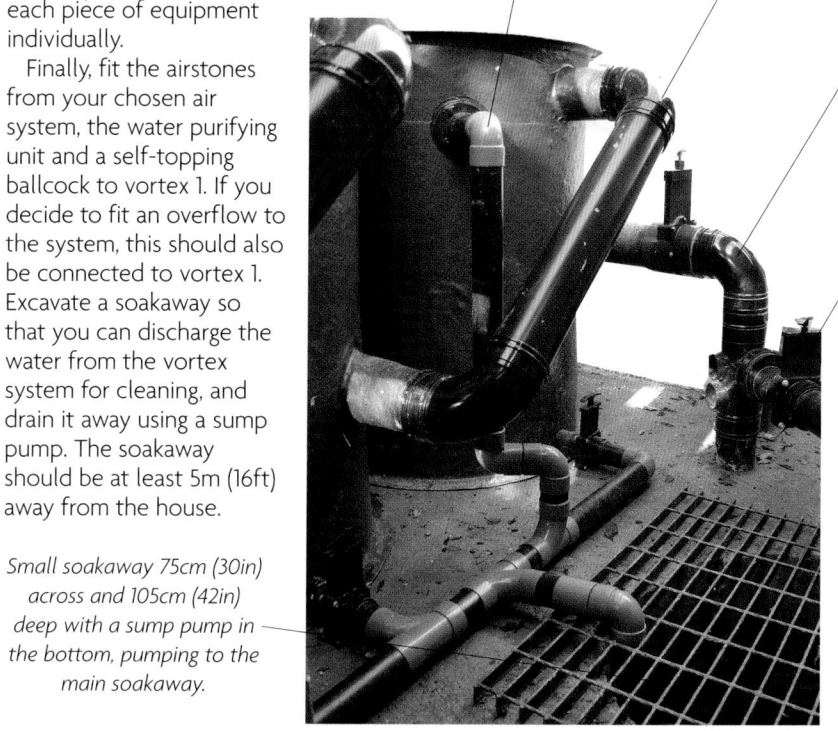

Right: The pump receives water from the third vortex chamber and from the surface skimmer and pumps it via the UV clarifier and heater back to the pond.

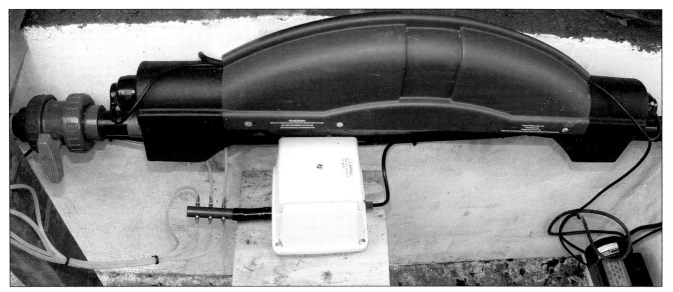

Below: These are the pump returns shown in the finished fibreglassed pond. Before fibreglassing, the protruding pipes are cut as flush as possible with the walls to reduce the number of obstacles in the pond for the fish to damage themselves on. These pipes are then rubbed down on both the outside and inside to create a key for the fibreglass.

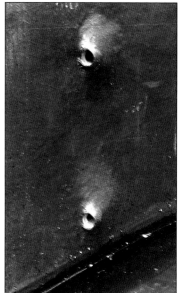

Above: The UV clarifier installed. A double union ball valve has been fitted before and after the unit, so that the water flow through it can be stopped and the unit removed by undoing one of the unions on each of the valves. The airpump for the pond can also be seen, with the airline running from it to wherever you wish the air to be delivered. In this system the airpump could be located above, or at the same level as the water in the pond. If the pump is located below water level, fit non-return valves to stop any water back siphoning down the airlines in the event of a power cut.

Left: These are the two pump returns to the pond seen from the filter bay side. A ball valve installed on each pipe allows the flow balance between them to be adjusted or each can be shut off. Notice the 45° angle at which the 38mm (1.5in) pipes passes through the pond wall.

The best way to provide a waterproof seal is to treat the internal walls of the pond with fibreglass. Render the walls first and shape the floor with render in a neat, even spiral down to the bottom drain. Add fibre mix to the render to strengthen it.

To fibreglass the pond, apply a layer of resin to an area of wall, followed by one sheet of fibreglass matting. Continue round the pond in this way, overlapping the sheets of matting by 5-7.5cm (2-3in). When two sheets have been laid, place an additional sheet overlapping each sheet by a half. Finally, apply a third layer of resin using a paddle roller to stipple and ensure an even spread. It is a good idea to carry out this procedure when the ambient temperature is above 15°C (59°F) so that the resin can cure completely.

Allow the fibreglassing to dry out for 24 hours and then thoroughly rub down the entire area with sandpaper to remove any rough edges and burs. When you are happy with the surface, apply an even layer of coloured top coat. Make sure that the top coat is applied in one continuous process.

How to fibreglass a pond

1 Coat the rendered pond wall with resin and apply a sheet of chopped strand fibreglass matting.

2 Apply firm and even pressure with a roller impregnated with resin to fix the sheet in place.

3 Make sure that the matting adheres to the curved surfaces, here near the base of the pond.

Right: *This sample of 300gm/m² chopped strand matting clearly shows the structure of the fibreglass material. Wear protective gloves and, ideally, a face mask when handling any form of fibreglass and resin.*

4 Use a paddle roller to release any air trapped within the matting. The surface will be getting very sticky at this stage.

Completing the edges

1 It is vital to finish off the edges of the the pond cleanly and effectively. Ensure that the top edge around the pond has an overlap margin of 5-7.5cm (2-3in).

2 Make sure that the turned-over edge of matting is thoroughly drenched with resin by repeated application of the impregnated roller.

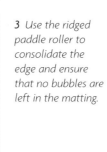

3 Use the ridged paddle roller to consolidate the edge and ensure that no bubbles are left in the matting.

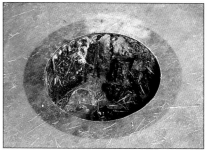

Left: Make sure that plastic skimmers and bottom drains are etched with sandpaper before fibreglassing to ensure a good key.

Above: The flange of the bottom drain is clearly visible through the layers of glassfibre matting used on the internal surfaces of this pond.

Below: The surface skimmer after fibreglassing, with all the edges smoothed off.

Above: Apply a top coat to the fibreglassed surface to complete the internal walls of the pond. Make sure that you complete this in one application.

Block-built pond – the finishing touches

Once the pond is finished, wait at least 48 hours before washing it out and discharging the water. This will remove any residues of cement, fibreglass or anything else that may prove hazardous to your fish before you introduce them.

When you fill the pond for the first time, use a water meter so that you can make a note of the exact capacity. This will be important later on if you need to treat the fish with any medication, when accurate dosing is crucial. Although you can buy a water meter, many koi dealers hire them for a small charge, which is ideal for a one-time use.

If you intend to put fish in the pond straightaway, you should add a biofilter startup chemical to the filter system. At this early stage, there will be no beneficial bacteria present in the filter to break down ammonia and the resultant nitrites produced as waste products by the fish. The biofilter startup chemical will speed up the maturation of the filter medium so that it begins to cleanse the water. Ideally, though, it is far better to fill the pond and allow it to run for 48 to 72 hours before introducing any fish, as this will allow the water to reach the ambient or heated temperature, and any excess chlorine will be dispersed. After this period, you can add one or two fish every few days. This avoids overloading the new filter and gives it time to adapt to the increasing waste loads being placed upon it. It is still a good idea to use a biofilter startup, even if you adopt this preferred method. Furthermore, if the water has not passed through a purifier, treat it with a suitable dechlorinator to remove chlorine, chloramine and metals.

Above: The block-built pond nearing completion. The filtration systems are housed under wooden decking, with trapdoors to provide easy access. Notice how the untidy blockwork is now completely hidden by the face brickwork.

Left: Follow the instructions when using dechlorinating water conditioners. Add the dose you need to a watering can of pond water and sprinkle it onto the pond surface or into the surface skimmer.

The decorative surfaces

In this design, the filter area is disguised using wooden decking, with doors to provide essential access to the filter system. This provides a pleasant seating area from which to observe and enjoy the fish. When installing decking, be sure to use tanalised timber that will withstand the elements for up to 20 years.

Finish off the external pond wall in a material that suits both the house and the rest of the garden. Backfill the edge of the pond with sand and soil so that the grass will grow again.

The material you choose for the top edge of the external wall is a matter of personal preference. Here it has been topped with slate, which produces a superb, natural appearance. To achieve a perfect fit, make a template and cut each piece of slate to the exact size. Number the pieces so that they fit together correctly, and secure them with a suitable adhesive.

The completed pond

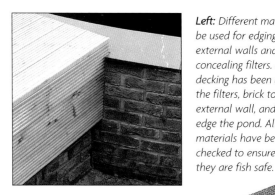

Left: Different materials can be used for edging, hiding external walls and concealing filters. Here, decking has been used over the filters, brick to hide the external wall, and slate to edge the pond. All these materials have been checked to ensure that they are fish safe.

Do not cover the top of the skimmer with pond edging (or make it removable) because you will need access to empty the collecting basket.

Paving slabs or rocks are generally used to finish the pond edge. It is best to use an impervious material because it will not allow any water to pass through it. If you do use a permeable rock or other material, seal it to reduce the risk of it leaking into the pond. Also seal any cement used to hold down the slabs/rocks around the pond for the same reason.

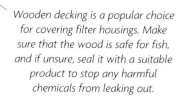

Wooden decking is a popular choice for covering filter housings. Make sure that the wood is safe for fish, and if unsure, seal it with a suitable product to stop any harmful chemicals from leaking out.

The exterior wall of the pond is finished in brick, but anything could be used, from plain render to logroll. Whatever material you use for the outside does not have to be treated as there is no risk of it leaking harmful substances into the pond.

Part Three

Maintaining your koi pond

Your pond is built, your koi are swimming around happily in their new home and you can sit back and relax – wrong! Now that your pond is up and running, you will need to devise a routine for yourself so that you can regularly carry out all the tasks required to keep your system in optimum condition. Some jobs, such as feeding the fish and testing the water, obviously apply to every pond, whereas others depend on the type of filtration you have installed. In this part of the book, we start by looking at the maintenance of a pump-fed system and then go on to examine the care of a gravity-fed pond.

This is followed by a more detailed discussion of important topics that are appropriate no matter what type of pond you have, such as feeding, monitoring the health of the fish and water testing. You will soon realise that all these aspects of koi-keeping are inextricably linked with the efficient running of the pond, however large or small it is and regardless of the complexity of the systems you have installed. For that reason, you should make them part of the everyday regime of dealing with your pond. Set aside a certain time each day to check filters and appliances and to carry out the necessary maintenance quickly. While your fish are feeding, look them over and keep an eye open for potential problems. Dedicate yourself to these tasks and you, your pond and your koi will undoubtedly enjoy the benefits in the long run.

So that is it, you are thinking. But there is one last thing to think about and that is how to improve your pond. The systems described in the book so far will more than adequately support a koi community, but in this part of the book we look at some items of equipment that you may wish to add to your pond at a later date. One example is a water purifier. Including one of these during the initial setting up process will confer undoubted benefits, but the absence of a purifier will not affect the basic functioning of the pond. It is an item you can add later, so it is discussed in this part of the book. So read this final section and get ready to start making those inevitable alterations that are all part of the ongoing enjoyment of the hobby.

Here we look at the specific tasks that together make up a maintenance regime that will keep a pump-fed pond in good condition. Following these recommendations will ensure that your pond provides a healthy and stable environment for your fish. If you have 'upgraded' your pond with extra systems such as heating, surface skimmers and aeration, then check the advice given for a gravity-fed system to see how they will fit into your maintenance timetable.

Daily
Feed fish The fundamental task for every koi-keeper is to feed the fish. However, this should be one of the most rewarding aspects of the hobby and not merely a chore.

Check fish Feeding the fish gives you an opportunity to check their general health and behaviour, and spot any potential problems as soon as they develop.

Check appliances Monitoring the vital equipment that keeps the pond functioning efficiently will alert you to any malfunctions before they have a major effect on the pond.

Weekly
Clean the pump In pump-fed systems, the pump is in the pond, where it continuously draws dirty water into the filter system. If the pump has a sponge prefilter, clean this at least once a week — even more frequently during the summer months. If you are using a pump designed to pump solids, it will not

need cleaning so often. Even so, it is a good idea to take your pump out of the pond once a week and clean it whatever its condition.

Clean the mechanical filter media Most pump-fed filter systems have a compartment containing a mechanical medium, such as foam or brushes, that will trap suspended solids. The amount of solids entering the filter will depend on the pump you are using — one with a prefilter will pass on less solids than one without. It is important that you only clean out the mechanical stage of your filter on a

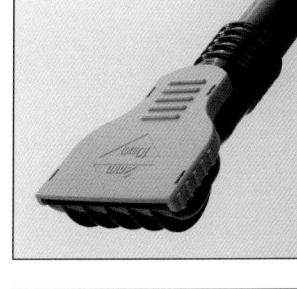

Left: The suction nozzle is adjustable to draw up sludge and debris of different grades. At this setting the nozzle will take in particles up to 2mm (0.08in) across.

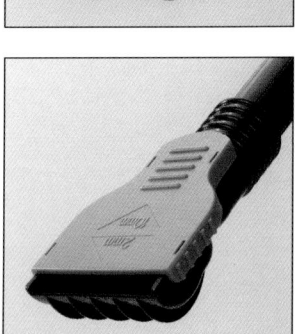

Left: Here the nozzle has been adjusted to take in debris up to 10mm (0.4in) across. For thin layers of mud, turning the nozzle over can prove effective.

Pond sludge is discharged though this tube.

Extension tubes allow the suction nozzle to reach into deep ponds.

Above: *Pond vacuum cleaners such as this can be used to remove sludge and debris from the pond floor or filter. The waste collects in the unit before being discharged to waste.*

weekly basis; do not disturb the beneficial bacteria in the biological sections. At the same time as you clean the mechanical media, take the opportunity to discharge any waste from the filter if your system has the facility to do this.

Test the water You cannot tell just by looking at the water whether it is safe for the fish. Choose from the many water testing kits available on the market and stick to the same ones for consistent results.

Monthly
Vacuum clean the pond Waste will collect on the bottom of a pump-fed pond and the best way to remove it is to use a pond vacuum cleaner. If you leave the waste it will decompose and cause poor water quality, which could lead to health problems. Most vacuum devices pump water out of the pond during the cleaning process. This is not a bad thing, because a water change of up to 20% is beneficial. Cleaning the pond regularly will not only reduce the waste, but in the longer term it will actually cut down the time spent vacuuming and the resultant water loss. Replacing more than 20% of the water may cause stress to the fish and affect the biological health of the filter system.

Half-yearly
Change the UV tube If you are using a UV clarifier to control green water, be sure to change the UV tube every six months. To be effective, the tube needs to be working at 100% light output and this can normally only be guaranteed in the first six months of its life.

Yearly
Give your filter system a complete clean out once a year. Stagger the process by cleaning out separate sections of the filter on different weeks. And be sure to use pond water to clean the biological media. Otherwise, you may reduce the populations of beneficial bacteria.

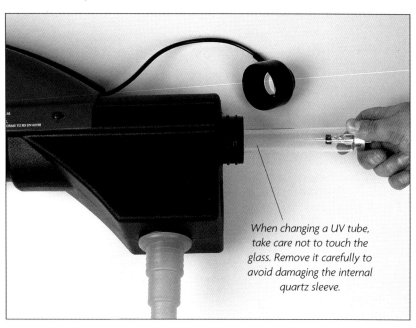

When changing a UV tube, take care not to touch the glass. Remove it carefully to avoid damaging the internal quartz sleeve.

Pump-fed maintenance schedule

	Daily	Weekly	Monthly	Half yearly	Yearly
Feed the fish					
Check fish					
Check appliances					
Clean pump					
Clean media					
Test water					
Vacuum pond					
Change UV lamp					
Clean out filter system					

Left: UV bulbs only last at the strength needed to stop green water for six months. Keep a record of when you change the bulb. It will still light after this time but will not be very effective.

Essential maintenance for a gravity-fed pond is the same as for a pump-fed one, plus the extra attention needed for any additional systems, such as surface skimmers, heating, aeration, vortex chambers, etc.

Daily
Feed and check fish, check appliances Follow the general advice on page 62 and refer to the sections on feeding and health care for more details.

Discharge the vortex and filters On a gravity-fed system, all the waste is carried to the filter through the drain at the bottom of the pond. This exposes the filter to a large amount of waste, which if left in

Purging the bottom drain

Follow this sequence to remove heavy waste items that settle in the pipe from the bottom drain to the filter.

1 Turn off the pump
2 Shut off the 110mm (4in) valve to the filter
3 Open the waste valve on the first chamber
4 Wait for the chamber to empty
5 When it is empty, open the 110mm (4in) valve, as shown at right
6 Allow the chamber to refill
7 Leave the chamber for 5-10 minutes
8 Open the waste valve on the first chamber to remove the waste

the filter would create problems and eventually block the system. It is vital to remove this waste. On a gravity-fed system, cleaning out a particular chamber or vortex, if fitted, is simply a matter of opening the relevant valves and flushing the waste to the main drain. Before you open any valves, turn off the pump, UV clarifier and any other appliances in the circuit. Restore the power to these units once the drained chambers have filled up again and the water level is high enough not to leave the pump running dry.

If you do have a vortex chamber, then you will find that most of the waste accumulates here and flushing this out every day will make daily discharging of the subsequent filter chambers unnecessary. Even so, it is advisable to discharge all the media chambers at least once a week.

Weekly
Purge the bottom drain Because a large-bore pipe connects the bottom pond drain to the filter, the water flow through it is quite slow. This means that large, heavy chunks of

waste may settle in the pipe and not reach the filter at all. To move this waste it is important to purge the bottom drain pipe once a week. To do this, first close the valve to isolate the pond from the filter and drain the vortex or first filter chamber. Then open the pond drain valve and a massive surge of water will flow into the empty chamber, bringing with it any waste in the pipe. Leave the waste to settle for a few minutes before discharging it to the main drain.

Clean the surface skimmers The frequency of cleaning out the surface skimmer will vary according to the time of year. In the autumn, for example, fallen leaves are likely to cause the biggest blockage in the collecting basket. At any rate, check the skimmer every week and empty the basket if necessary.

Clean the mechanical filter media If you have brushes in the first filter chamber, then clean these every week in the same way as on a pump-fed pond.

Test the water Refer to the section on water quality (page 70) for details on testing.

Monthly
Check and adjust water temperature If you are heating your pond, monitor the temperature every day. However, it will be on a month-by-month basis that you will need to adjust the temperature. In temperate regions, it is beneficial to koi to bring the temperature down slightly in the autumn and raise it

again in spring. As the autumn approaches, gradually lower the temperature if you wish to a minimum of 13 or 14°C (55 or 57°F) by allowing a drop of 1°C (2-3°F) every two or three days. This will allow the koi's immune system to remain functioning and avoid many of the problems associated with a lower water temperature. At the onset of spring, progressively raise the temperature to 18°C (64°F) or above. (Adjusting the temperature in 1°C steps reduces the stress caused by larger changes in temperature.)

Adjust aeration Temperature and aeration go hand-in-hand. More aeration is required in the warm summer months (oxygen is less soluble in warm water) and less aeration is needed in the cold winter months. It is best to reduce or cease the aeration of unheated ponds during the winter anyway, because it will draw cold air into the pond and bring the water temperature down even further. For the same reason, decrease or shut down waterfalls and venturis during the cold winter period.

Half yearly
Change the UV tube As for a pump-fed pond.

Yearly
Clean the filter system Since the filter chambers are regularly discharged to waste, a gravity-fed filter system should not need such a drastic annual overhaul as a pump-fed one.

If you check the media chambers and they do not appear to be dirty, leave the relevant discharge valve open for a while so that pond water flows over the media and carries any waste to the main drain. This process can be helped by pouring pond water over the media to dislodge any waste not removed. Leave the discharge valve open as you do this.

Right: A floating pond thermometer to monitor pond temperature. Some models have a colour zone to indicate the temperature range within which koi are able to accept food.

Below: A multichamber filter system, with brushes and matting in view. Notice how the brushes collect debris from the incoming flow of pond water and thus need regular cleaning.

Gravity-fed maintenance

	Daily	Weekly	Monthly	Half yearly	Yearly
Feed the fish					
Check fish					
Check appliances					
Discharge vortex					
Discharge filters					
Check water temperature					
Purge bottom drain					
Clean surface skimmers					
Clean media					
Test water					
Adjust water temperature					
Adjust aeration					
Change UV lamp					
Clean out filter system					

Feeding your koi

Feeding your koi will become one of the most enjoyable aspects of your hobby, and gives you a chance to appreciate the fish at least once a day (although this is not the best year-round feeding regime – see page 68). The amount and type of food you give your koi will largely depend on the water temperature. If the pond is heated to a minimum of 14°C (57°F) all year round, you have the advantage of being able to feed the fish throughout the year. Not only will this enable you to watch them all year round, but it also helps you to achieve amazing growth rates. If the pond is not heated, monitor the

Right: Koi are totally dependent on their owners for food. They need a good-quality, varied diet that takes into account water temperature, and the size, weight and number of fish in the pond. Overfeeding puts a heavy load on the filtration system.

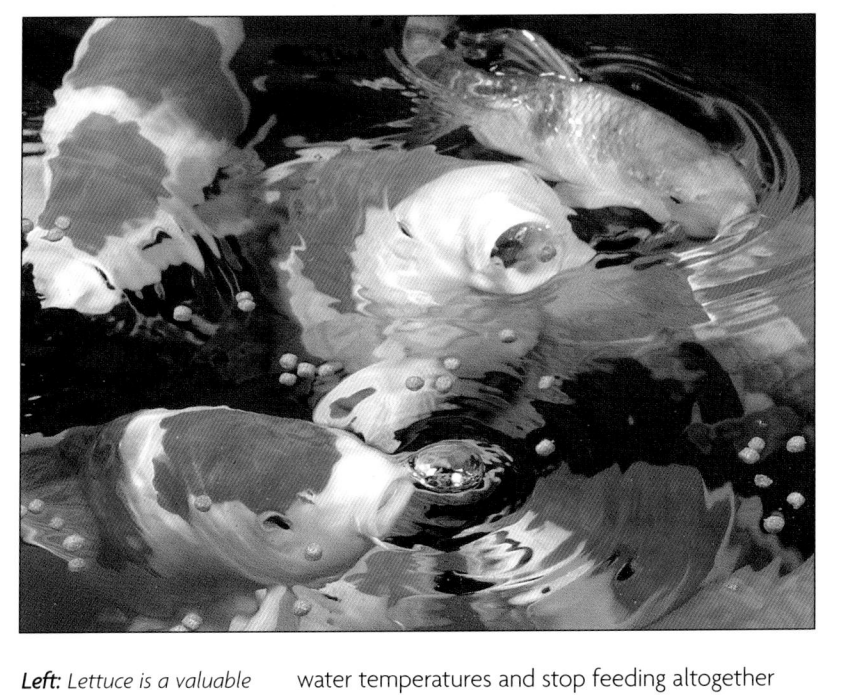

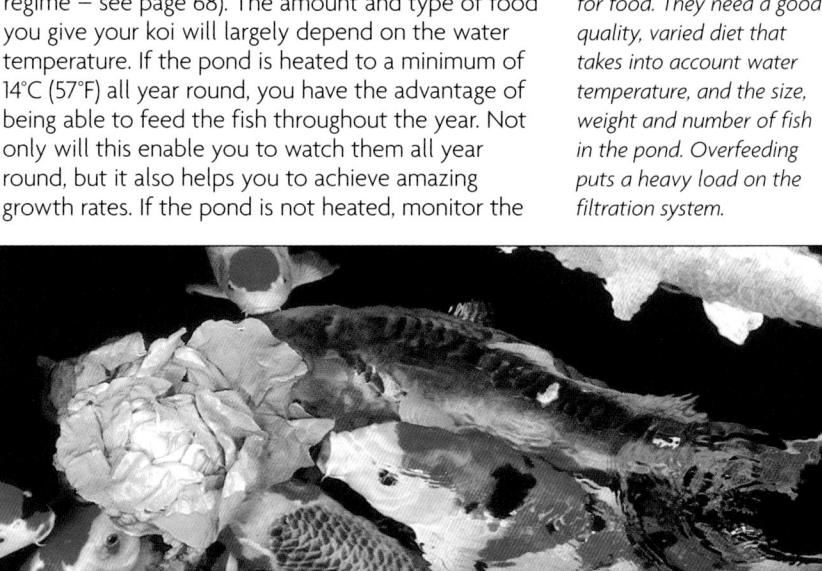

Left: Lettuce is a valuable source of Vitamin C and other nutrients. Start by offering shredded leaves; in a short time, the koi will enjoy chasing a whole lettuce around the pond and tearing off pieces. Oranges are another treat, but remove uneaten items before they decompose.

water temperatures and stop feeding altogether when it drops below 8°C (46°F). In water temperatures of 8-14°C (46-57°F), offer the koi a lower-protein food, such as wheatgerm, which they can digest more easily. At temperatures above 14°C (57°F), feed them on a standard staple food, and in the very warmest months, add specialist colour or growth-enhancing foods.

Koi food is available in all shapes and sizes, from sticks and pellets to paste and even sinking varieties. The type of food you give your koi is a matter of

Dried foods

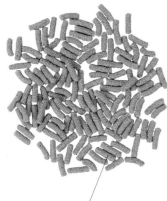

Pellets containing spirulina algae are thought to enhance a koi's red coloration.

Right: Pelleted, flake and other dried foods provide koi with a well-balanced diet. However, formulations vary, so check the ingredients carefully. Store food in airtight containers and do not carry them over from one season to the next.

These floating sticks contain protein to encourage growth and reproduction in summer.

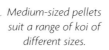

Medium-sized pellets suit a range of koi of different sizes.

Oranges provide Vitamin C. The koi will cluster eagerly round the segments, eating everything but the peel.

Small pellets are suitable for young koi. There is a wide range of proprietary foods from which to choose.

Large pellets for adult koi. Offer your koi the right size food so they can swallow it easily.

Above: Wholemeal or granary bread is a good source of wheatgerm and vitamins, but it is rich in carbohydrate so feed it sparingly. Peas and sweetcorn are also high-carbohydrate foods that make the fish excessively fat.

67

personal choice, but bear in mind that as in most things, you get what you pay for in terms of quality.

The most popular types of food include floating pellets and sticks, which are widely available. Many different ingredients are included in these foods, all designed to improve the health, condition and colour of your fish. Several food additives are available that provide further nutritional benefits.

When feeding your koi it is best to offer them small amounts several times a day, rather than one or two large feeds. As a guide, provide enough food so that none is left after three to five minutes. In the colder months a single feed each day will be sufficient, but in the hotter summer months you can feed the fish four or five times a day, as well as offering treats such as prawns and oranges. Adding some sinking food to the staple diet encourages the koi to feed at different levels in the pond, thus reducing the risk of your prize koi damaging each other when they all rush to the surface.

Preparing paste food

1 This food is supplied as a fine powder. Follow the instructions and measure out the amount needed to make one day's food ration.

2 Using the supplied measuring cup for convenience, slowly add enough tapwater to the powder to make it moist but not too wet.

3 Mix the powder and water together until it has a dough-like consistency. Add more water as needed to create a soft paste.

Left: *Young koi chasing an orange segment around the surface of their pond. They will eat the flesh of the fruit with enthusiasm until only the clean peel remains. Remove this to prevent it rotting in the water.*

4 Knead the paste in your hands and peel off lumps of food to feed your koi. Make the pieces in a suitable size for your koi and simply throw them in the pond.

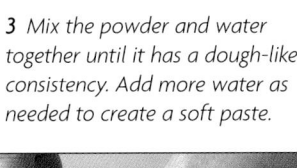

Mixing an additive with koi food

1 Measure out enough feed for one or two days. This is a staple pelleted food suitable for everyday feeding.

2 Add water to the food to make it just moist. This will help it to absorb the additive more effectively.

3 Stir the food to ensure that it all comes into contact with the water. Use a large bowl to prevent spillage.

4 Measure out the appropriate amount of the additive being used. This one confers health, colour-enhancing and growth benefits.

5 Mix the food thoroughly to ensure an even covering of the additive. Then leave food for a few minutes to allow the additive to soak in and the pellets to dry out.

6 Feed the treated food to your koi but ensure that it is used within one or two days. This is to ensure that it is fresh and the full benefits are gained.

General maintenance – water quality

At the very least, test your pond water for ammonia, nitrite and pH every week. Most problems arise in some way from poor water quality and regular testing enables you to pinpoint irregularities quickly so that you can take any necessary remedial action. Try to get into the habit of regular water testing and, ideally, also include tests for dissolved oxygen level (particularly in warm weather), nitrate and general water hardness.

How the nitrogen cycle works

Water returning to the pond from the last stage of the filtration system may still contain some nitrate. Nitrate is one of the nutrients responsible for promoting the growth of blanketweed.

Water changes are an important aspect of pond management, especially if ammonia or nitrite are polluting the pond. Regular water changes can also help to reduce nitrate concentration in the water.

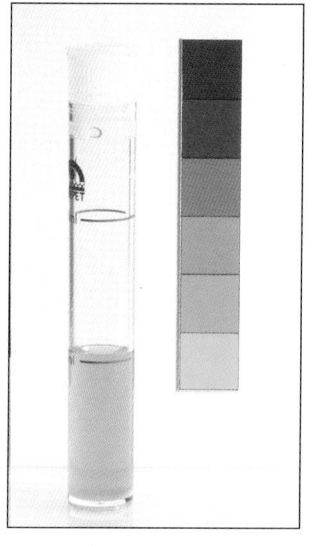

Above: To test pond water for the presence of ammonia, compare a sample against the colours on the chart supplied.

By adding an oxygen atom into each molecule, aerobic bacteria (Nitrobacter spp.) convert nitrite into nitrate (NO_3). Nitrate is the final breakdown product of ammonia in the nitrogen cycle and far less toxic than ammonia or nitrite.

Protein supplied in food is used by koi for tissue repair and maintenance, growth and reproduction. Any excess protein cannot be stored and is excreted as ammonia. The protein in any uneaten food also ends up as ammonia.

By removing the hydrogen and adding oxygen into each molecule, aerobic bacteria (Nitrosomonas spp.) convert ammonia into nitrite (NO_2). Although not as harmful as ammonia, is still poisonous to koi.

Ammonia (NH_3) is released into the water by the gills. The small amount of urea voided in dilute urine breaks down to form ammonia. Ammonia is very poisonous to koi.

Broad range pH test

Above: It is vital to test the pH of the water routinely, as this affects the toxicity of ammonia. The ideal pH range for the koi pond is between 6.5 and 8.5, so a broad range test kit is ideal. Here, a small tablet is mixed with 10ml of pond water and the colour compared to a chart.

Nitrite test

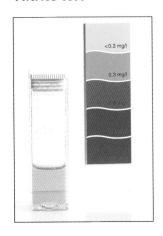

Left: Nitrite, the secondary breakdown product of ammonia, is also poisonous to koi. High levels often occur in new ponds before the nitrogen cycle is established. Monitor the pond and carry out partial water changes.

pH 4 Too acidic – koi unwell, not feeding. Hard water: increase pH by water changes. Soft water: partial water changes, add marble chippings, oyster shell or chalk-based minerals/clays.

pH 5 pH still too low – koi will be lethargic. Increase pH as described above.

pH 6.5 Preferred pH range is 6.5-8.5, but even at this level, it could be increased.

pH 7 Pure or distilled water is pH 7, but unlikely to be achieved in the koi pond. Distilled water is devoid of minerals/salts.

pH 8.5 Top value recommended for koi. Does not cause them any major problems.

pH 9 In planted ponds, or those affected by algae blooms, pH can rise above 9 to about 11 during the day, but causes few welfare or health problems.

Dissolved oxygen test

Oxygen is essential for koi and a number of factors, including water temperature and the number of fish in the pond, can adversely affect dissolved oxygen levels.

2 Swirl the solution until it is an even colour.

3 Add the final reagent one drop at a time.

1 Stabilise the oxygen content by adding a series of reagents. At this point, a further reagent causes the test sample to turn black.

4 Count the drops until the solution is clear for the oxygen reading.

Make a habit of checking your koi every day at feeding time. This will enable you to see that they are all present and behaving normally. When they come up to the surface you can inspect them closely them for any signs of damage or disease. If there seems to be a general disease problem, you can dose the whole pond with a suitable treatment. The presence of parasites, for example, may be indicated by the fish flicking against the bottom or sides of the pond.

General anti-parasite treatments are available; always follow the manufacturer's guidance on dosing rates. You must measure out these medications accurately, taking into account the exact volume of your pond; make sure you know what it is. If you underdose, the medication simply will not work and overdosing may have a harmful effect on the koi. Buy a good measuring cylinder or set of gram balances to measure out the appropriate medication, be it liquid or powder. If possible, take a mucus scrape from an affected fish and examine it under a microscope to determine the exact parasite. This allows you to select the best medication.

If just one or two koi have raised or lost scales or small wounds, this may indicate that there is an area or

Below: *Pond medications are strong chemicals and it is vital that you measure the amount accurately to ensure that you give the correct dose. Mix it with some pond water before adding the diluted treatment to your pond.*

Simple microscope

Single-lens eyepiece

Adjustment wheel to bring image into focus

Three objective lenses for different magnifications

Stage with retaining clips to hold slide

Movable mirror reflects light through the glass slide

Left: *This entry-level microscope offers all the functions needed to identify problems such as parasites.*

object in the pond on which the fish are damaging themselves. Carefully take out the affected fish and treat any wounds individually. If the fish is large or awkward to handle, you may need to anaesthetise it to reduce the levels of stress involved. Find out how the damage occurred and take steps to prevent it happening again. Raised or lost scales may reflect damage caused by flicking due to parasites or an increased level of bacteria in the pond, in which case more general treatment of the water is necessary. If you experience this, seek professional advice, as a bacterial swab may need to be taken and cultured to determine the exact problem.

Below: Hand-feeding gives you the ideal opportunity to examine your fish. Make sure they are all present and feeding well, and check them over for skin damage, parasitic infestation or other abnormalities.

Treating a koi with propolis

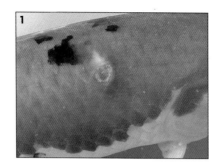

1 A typical small wound or ulcer on koi.

2 Anaesthetise the koi and carefully clean the affected site with a cotton wool bud.

3 Treat the cleaned area with propolis spray until it is fully covered. This will be absorbed into the surface tissues, not only disinfecting the area but also stopping bacteria further penetrating the tissues.

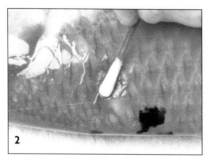

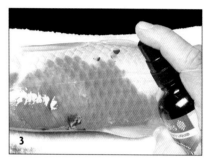

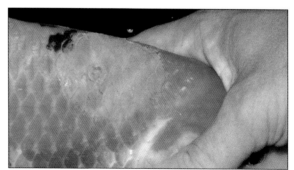

Left: Allow the propolis to dry and form a protective coating over the affected area. Then place the koi back into the pond in a floating basket near an airstone. Repeat every two to three days, or as needed. If problems persist, seek expert help.

No matter how well you have planned your pond, there will always be ways of improving it by adding extra pieces of equipment or making changes to improve its efficiency. We have considered some of these options on pages 28-33. Here, we look at other ways to improve and enhance your pond system, even after it has been completed.

Automatic top-up system
Whatever type of pond you have, there will be times when you need to discharge water from it and fill it back up to the original level. Normally, you would use a hosepipe to do this, but there is an easier option: fit an automatic top-up system. These are based on the mechanisms that refill the cistern on a water closet. A float rises and falls with the pond level and is connected to a valve on the mains water feed pipe. If the level falls, the float drops and water flows into the pond until the float reaches a preset level and turns off the supply. Although you can fit a top-up system anywhere in the pond, it is best to keep it out of sight – under a bridge crossing the pond is a good place. On a gravity-fed pond, you can fit an automatic top-up system in the filter. This is not possible on a pump-fed pond because the filter is at a different level to the pond.

If you are using an automatic top-up system it is vital to fit an overflow pipe that will prevent the pond overfilling and flooding the filters and the garden. In fact, it is a good idea even if you fill the pond by hand.

Water purification unit
In addition to a range of naturally occurring substances, mains drinking water contains chlorine and/or chloramine to make it safe for human consumption. For koi pond use, it is important to dispel these water treatment chemicals and one way of doing this is to add a liquid dechlorinator to the new incoming water. An easier and automatic alternative is to fit a water purification unit. These contain cartridges that remove a range of substances from the tapwater as it passes through, including

Left: This automatic top-up unit is connected to the mains water supply and the float set to the water level. When the level drops, the lowered floats allows mains water to flow in until the float returns to its original position.

Above: Water purifiers will remove many if not all the substances found in tapwater that are harmful to fish. Choose the size of unit you need based on how much water you will change per week, month and year.

chlorine and chloramine. Since the level of these chemicals and natural substances varies from area to area, be sure to check with your local water company so that you can buy the most appropriate purification cartridges to treat your tapwater.

The right size of purification unit will not depend on your pond volume so much as the amount of water you need to treat. Units vary in the treatment capacity they offer before the cartridges need changing. It is a good idea to install a water meter after the unit so that you can monitor the volume of water passing through it and keep a note of when the cartridges need replacing. The ideal combination would be an automatic top-up plus a purification unit, providing a completely hands-free water refilling system.

Filter modifications

You can upgrade and modify your filter system in a number of ways to improve your whole pond system. If you have a pump-fed pond, the most obvious upgrade is to change to a gravity-fed filter system. Clearly, this is not an easy and quick process, but it will give you improved waste removal and great flexibility in filter layout and design.

With gravity-fed systems, adding extra filter units to your existing setup is always worth considering, because you can never have too much filtration capacity. You can also switch to newer 'advanced' types of media that provide more efficient biological filtration. And if you do not have a vortex already, consider adding one at the beginning of your filter system to replace that massive chamber filled with brushes.

At the same time, consider fitting a mechanical strainer to the filter system. One type of highly engineered mechanical strainer consists of a stainless steel cylinder that fits on the outlet pipe taking water from the vortex or the first chamber receiving pond water to the rest of the filter. The unit actually fits inside the vortex or chamber, surrounded by the raw pond water with its suspended waste. An integrated pump pulls water through the fine mesh that runs around the edge, filtering out even the finest particles. To keep the mesh unblocked, part of the pumped water flow is directed back into the cylinder and through a rotor arm with angled slots that spray water against the mesh from the inside. The angled water jets keep the rotor arm spinning as it cleans the strainer mesh.

The advantage of such a self-cleaning mechanical strainer is that it significantly reduces the amount of solid waste that reaches the subsequent filter chambers, thus improving their efficiency. Another benefit is that it will keep most of the pond waste in one chamber, and this can be cleared by discharging just this single chamber. Other plus points include improved water clarity and quality, low maintenance, healthier conditions, and the ease with which such a unit can be fitted to either a pump-fed or gravity-fed filter system.

Keep an open mind

If you become absorbed in the koi hobby, it is unlikely that the first pond you build will be your last. And you will always want to improve the current setup you have. Some improvements can be very simple ones. Just adding switchboxes or remotely controlled switchboxes so that all your electrical appliances are connected to one control unit can streamline your day-to-day tasks enormously. Do look for ways to upgrade and improve your pond, but keep an open mind and a watchful eye on new advances as they become available. Some may indeed be the answer to your prayers; others may be gimmicks that offer you no advancement at all.

Cylindrical mechanical strainer

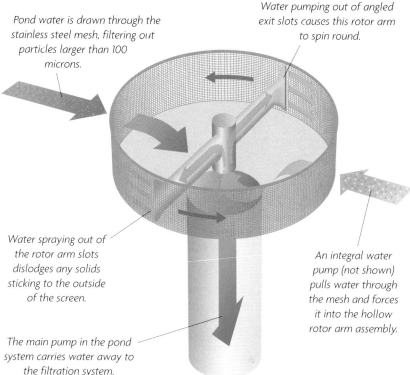

Pond water is drawn through the stainless steel mesh, filtering out particles larger than 100 microns.

Water pumping out of angled exit slots causes this rotor arm to spin round.

Water spraying out of the rotor arm slots dislodges any solids sticking to the outside of the screen.

An integral water pump (not shown) pulls water through the mesh and forces it into the hollow rotor arm assembly.

The main pump in the pond system carries water away to the filtration system.

INDEX

Page numbers in **bold** indicate major entries; *italics* refer to captions and annotations; plain type indicates other text entries.

CREDITS

Practical photographs by Geoffrey Rogers © Interpet Publishing.

The publishers would like to thank the following photographers for providing images, credited here by page number and position: B(Bottom), T(Top), C(Centre), BL(Bottom Left), etc.

Dave Bevan: 10(TR), 15(TL), 34, 37(B), 45
David Brown: 36(T)
Eric Crichton: Title page, 6, 8, 9(L)
Terry Hill (The Koi Pond Konstruction Kompany.): 10(BL), 11(BR), 48(BL), 50(BR)
Keith Holmes: 48(T, BR)
Marine World Publications Ltd.: 11(BL, Colin and Thelma Shaw), 11 (TR, Gwyn and Maureen Davis), 12 (Richard and Donna Jones), 13(TL, Bob Lewis), 13 (BR), 27(BL)
Darren Metalli: 47(BR), 59(TC)

Computer graphics by Phil Holmes and Stuart Watkinson © Interpet Publishing.

The publishers would like to thank Koi Water Barn, Chelsfield Village, Kent for their help during the preparation of this book, particularly Tony, Keith, Ray, Darren, Paul, Colin and Andrew.

Thanks are also due to Andy Fletcher; Terry Hill, The Koi Pond Konstruction Kompany; NT Laboratories Ltd., Wateringbury, Kent; Nick Stansfield; Tetra UK, Eastleigh, Hampshire.